P9-DER-099

ACCLAIM FOR *OFF THE RECORD*

"Meow-worthy anecdotes from celebrities ranging from Jada Pinkett Smith to Snoop Dogg and Shaq."
—*Sister 2 Sister Magazine*

"An appealing look at the stars and one reporter who covers them."
—*Booklist*

"The award-winning *Newsweek* correspondent . . . goes deep in this book of compelling essays about covering the entertainment industry. Her star tales are insightful, frank, funny and often surprising."
—*Heart & Soul*

"Samuels dishes on celeb interviewees like Denzel and Tyra."
—*People*

"Allison is one of the most respected journalists out there and one of the few I trust to talk to when something goes down. I know I'm going to get fair coverage when we deal."
—Sean "P. Diddy" Combs

"One of the best reporters/writers in the business. No one digs deeper for the real story."
—Denzel Washington

"Allison Samuels has been one of the most supportive journalists of my career. She makes a point of trying to understand her subject so the story has balance and does the person justice. As an artist you can't ask for more."
—Dr. Dre, award-winning hip-hop artist and producer

ALSO BY ALLISON SAMUELS

Christmas Soul:
African American Holiday Stories

OFF THE RECORD

A Reporter Unveils the Celebrity Worlds of
Hollywood, Hip-hop, and Sports

Allison Samuels

Amistad
An Imprint of HarperCollinsPublishers

A hardcover edition of this book was published in 2007 by
Amistad, an imprint of HarperCollins Publishers.

OFF THE RECORD. Copyright © 2007 by Allison Samuels.
All rights reserved. Printed in the United States of America.
No part of this book may be used or reproduced in any
manner whatsoever without written permission except in
the case of brief quotations embodied in critical articles
and reviews. For information address HarperCollins
Publishers, 10 East 53rd Street, New York, NY 10022.

HarperCollins books may be purchased for educational,
business, or sales promotional use. For information
please write: Special Markets Department, HarperCollins
Publishers, 10 East 53rd Street, New York, NY 10022.

First Amistad paperback edition published 2008.

Designed by Renato Stanisic

The Library of Congress has cataloged the hardcover
edition as follows:

Samuels, Allison.
    Off the record: a reporter unveils the celebrity worlds
of Hollywood, hip-hop, and sports / by Allison Samuels.
—1st ed.
    p.   cm.
  ISBN: 978-0-06-113766-2
  ISBN-10: 0-06-113766-9
    1. Entertainers—United States—Biography.
    2. Celebrities—United States—Biography. I. Title.

PN2285.S27 2007
791.092'273—dc22
[B]
                                                    2006048441

ISBN: 978-0-06-137435-7 (pbk.)

08 09 10 11 12 BVG/RRD 10 9 8 7 6 5 4 3 2

To my grandmothers, Classie Anderson and Loretta Samuels,
for always watching over me.

And to the late Mrs. Coretta Scott King
for being patient with me as a young journalist
and inspiring me beyond words.

Contents

11

Ballers and Shot Callers: Ray Lewis, Allen Iverson,
and A-Rod 148

12

Creepin' On Ah Come Up: Jodeci's DeVante Swing,
Tyra Banks, Bone Thugs-N-Harmony,
Lil' Kim, and Eminem 161

13

On Lockdown: Suge Knight and
Malcolm Shabazz in Prison 174

14

The Players Club:
A Behind-Closed-Doors World Where Hollywood,
Hip-hop, and Sports "Make It Rain" 183

##

A Journey Full Circle:
A Tribute to Coretta Scott King 189

Acknowledgments

What a blessing to be able to write this book. Oftentimes a reporter doesn't always reflect on how the stories they write might affect other people, much less themselves. Recounting my experiences of reporting over more than a decade reminds me how blessed I truly am.

Another blessing—Gilda Squire, my editor and confidante who saw this project from conception to completion. There are really no words!

To everyone at Amistad/HarperCollins—Dawn Davis, Rockelle Henderson, Christina Morgan, Yona Deshommes, Mark Jackson, Michael Morrison, Laura Klynstra, and all of the wonderful people on the sales team—I am grateful for all of your support and enthusiasm for this book.

My agent Luke Janklow—thank you for the inspiration and encouraging words.

I thank Mark Whitaker and the editors at *Newsweek* magazine for allowing me to spend the past thirteen years covering some of the most amazing people and events in the world.

To my boyz (and girlz) in the hood—Andre Young, Calvin Broadus, Shaquille O'Neal, and all my other subjects who made sure I never had a dull day or interview.

To my many friends and mentors who helped me get to this place in my life and career in one way or another— sometimes without even knowing it—Robert Watts, Zion and Dennis Banks, N'Croal, Marcus Mabry, Ann McDaniel, Mark Starr, Willie J. West, Chrissy Murray, and Marvet Britto. Thank you, thank you, thank you!!!

To James D. McJunkins, professor of journalism at Clark Atlanta University—everything I know about journalism I learned from you. Merci!

To my girls from my hometown of Augusta, Georgia— Dollie Williams Banks, Pammie Eagle Jimmar, and Carlotta Philo—who knew, right?

A special note of thanks to my many cousins, aunts, and uncles, and in particular, my auntie Sammie (Cassaundra Cain), for allowing me to type stories on her kitchen table until the wee hours of the night in college. Much love!

And last, but certainly not least, to my mother, Classie J. West, for being my one constant cheerleader no matter what was happening in my life. Couldn't have made it here without you! Love you tons!

OFF THE RECORD

Introduction

You can't get much of an interview with anyone without some sort of connection. I don't mean the right phone number or a perky mutual friend. I mean an emotional connection where a person chooses, for whatever reason, to let you in. Finding that connection isn't always immediate for a reporter, but it has to come at some point if there is to be any decent story. I never knew if I really had the ability to connect with a subject until the summer I met the legendary director Francis Ford Coppola on the set of his film *Gardens of Stone,* starring James Caan, Anjelica Huston, and James Earl Jones.

It was the mid-1980s, and Coppola had experienced his share of ups and downs, mainly the difficulty of matching the numbing success of the cult classic *The Godfather.* A family member of mine had a role in Coppola's new film and invited me to visit just for the fun of it. I planned to go a week before summer school began at Atlanta University Center so I could start off the semester with a bang. Then

came news of the death of Coppola's oldest son, Gian-
Carlo, in a tragic boating accident on the Washington,
D.C., set just a week before my trip. Though details were
sparse, information leaked out that the twenty-two-year-
old had been decapitated while joyriding with the son of
the actor Ryan O'Neal. I contemplated canceling my trip
when I heard the news, but filming was resuming, and I had
only one more week before school began.

Understandably, as soon as I arrived on the set of the
film, which focused on the lives of Vietnam vets, melancholy
and sadness shook me to my core. Although it was work as
usual, the cast, the crew, and the Coppola family were still
very much in shock, merely going through the motions. I
vividly recall Coppola often taking long breaks to gaze
blankly into the afternoon sky.

Given the vibe, I tried my best to tiptoe around the pro-
duction, hoping to stay out of the way and just learn as
much as I could about making a film. This was the first
movie location I'd been on, and since I'd planned on focus-
ing on entertainment journalism after college, I knew a lot
could be learned just from being near one of the most pro-
lific and brilliant directors of our time. As luck would have
it, I would have an opportunity to do more than observe the
director the day after I arrived. After I was introduced to
him, Coppola asked me why I wanted to become a journalist. I pondered the question for a moment, slightly surprised
that he even cared, and shot back, "I want to keep people
informed, with a different perspective." Simple, I know, but
it worked.

Something clicked at that moment, and Coppola invited

me into the editing trailer. There he pointed out the technology being used in the film and explained how most of it
would be out-of-date in the next ten years. Fortunately, I'd
brought a small notebook to jot down thoughts, and this
seemed a perfect moment to whip it out. As he spoke about
how film would change, Coppola also spoke of his loss and
how he'd hoped his eldest son would have been a part of
that change. Gian-Carlo had been a camera technician.

I wasn't sure what to say or why Coppola had chosen to
tell me any of this. I asked a few questions about his
son's plans, and the director seemed almost thankful to
share them with a complete stranger. It was this moment
which let me know that just maybe I had what it took to
become a journalist.

I took the short interview with Coppola and turned it
into a class paper that summer. My teacher found it moving
enough to suggest I submit it to the *Atlanta Journal-
Constitution*. Youth will allow you to do some pretty foolish
things. I convinced my girlfriend Pammie to ride the bus
with me to the downtown office of the newspaper so I could
present my hand-typed masterpiece to the entertainment
editor. The man's assistant looked at us as if we were aliens
just arriving on planet Earth as I handed her the brown
folder. It never occurred to me that the entertainment editor
of a major newspaper could care less about a black college
student's first real journalism piece, even if I had gotten an A
plus. Only at age eighteen would someone be this naïvely
bold. But it worked. The editor called me the next day in my
dorm room and offered me seventy-five dollars to print the
piece as well as an internship, which began immediately.

Although I was shocked at my good fortune, it had always been my dream. From the moment I saw a Barbara Walters interview when I was in grade school, I knew that was what I wanted to do. It also helped that I was the only child of a mother who taught second grade and who brought books home like candy. I'd spend my summers in our backyard in Augusta, Georgia, reading Judy Blume and Nancy Drew books until the sun went down.

However, it wasn't until the eighth grade that I realized the true power of the pen. My eighth-grade literature teacher, Mr. Buzzell, assigned me two books to read that would influence me to this day—*I Know Why the Caged Bird Sings* by Maya Angelou and *The Catcher in the Rye* by J. D. Salinger. Those two books showed me how words could jump off the page and take readers on a journey so real it was as if they were there. Though these books were beyond anything I could ever hope to write, I knew writing was my path.

Of course, there were detours. After completing a two-year internship with the *Los Angeles Times* following college, I left writing to work as a researcher for Quincy Jones's film company and eventually became an assistant for the director Robert Townsend, whom I met while interviewing him for the *Times*. At that time I was under the misguided idea that I wanted to do more than write about entertainment. I wanted to be a part of it.

I got a wake-up call in a hurry with my stint as an agent in training at the high and mighty Creative Artists Agency in Los Angeles during the days of Michael Ovitz, who ran Hollywood in the early 1990s. I can't tell you exactly how I became an agent in training. All I remember is going in to interview to become a reader (someone who reads scripts and writes summaries about them for the agents) and leaving with a spot as an agent trainee. My guess is that diversity was not plentiful among interviewees for the program, and with clients like John Singleton and Magic Johnson, they needed to make an attempt.

Either way, I got bamboozled into doing something that I wouldn't have chosen to do in a million years. They made it sound like *the* opportunity. Not. That is, not for me. Agent trainees spend their first months driving scripts around to studios and celebrities ten to twelve hours a day. My day would start at dawn, usually going to the store and preparing a made-to-order water for Michael Ovitz, who was always very sweet to me, and then move on to whatever else had to be done in the office before delivering the packages began.

One day, my task included blowing up about one hundred plastic dinosaurs for a visit by Steven Spielberg. He'd just released *Jurassic Park,* and the plastics dolls were to make him feel at home. It took two hours to blow up those dinosaurs for the atrium, and Spielberg's meeting lasted ten minutes. I was still catching my breath when the phone call came to "kill the dinosaurs." Had I really gone to college for this? Still, the bulk of my time was spent picking up Ted Danson's weekly half-million-dollar check for *Cheers* from the studio to take back to CAA for them to get their 10 percent before Danson saw it; or delivering *Friends* scripts to Courteney Cox, who always seemed scared to death of me when I'd approach her home. No wonder there were rarely any black people on *Friends.*

Yet there were those who were wonderful, like Sean

Penn, who met me at my car to get his packages, which was key because his home was at the top of a long-ass hill that I would have had to walk up if he hadn't been so gracious. He would even bring me treats like cold bottled water or ice-cream cones. A true class act. Then there was Dustin Hoffman, who quizzed me endlessly about my background and how I'd gotten to CAA. He seemed impressed, and I learned later he called to compliment them on hiring someone other than their best friends' children.

But those fond memories weren't enough to make me want to become an agent. Particularly after I took a script to the home of the director John Landis and got trapped in my car between two gates for hours before anyone inside noticed they hadn't pushed the button to let me out. I knew my days as an agent trainee had to be numbered. What a blessing that realization turned out to be, because on the horizon was the dawn of the hip-hop revolution, and that was where I wanted to be.

How Long Will They Mourn Me?

TUPAC SHAKUR

Tupac Shakur is chain-smoking, sitting in a chair, when I arrive for our interview one December afternoon in 1995. Glancing out the window of his hotel room off the Sunset Strip in Los Angeles, he bears little likeness to the hotheaded, fire-breathing hellion that he often becomes in his videos, in the courtroom, or on the local news. With the television blaring in the background, the twenty-four-year-old rapper's eyes dart around the room as the phone rings, his pager vibrates, and room service arrives in unison.

For all his bravado, Tupac Shakur could easily be confused with a nervous wreck of a man. He fiddles restlessly with his hands (his fingernails are bitten to the quick), can barely sit still, and speaks at warp speed, hardly taking a breath. "I just wanted to get out and go back to doing what I was meant to do, which is music," he told me that day. "I've been working nonstop because I had nothing but time, you know, to think about all the things I wanted to say on wax. You don't know what it's like to not be able to do what

you want, when you want. I had that for nine months. . . . I'm
making up for lost time."

Even though we've met a number of times before, he
sizes me up like I'm unfamiliar. I understand. Our previous
interviews all occurred at a much calmer time in his life,
when Tupac Shakur was a happier man. I'd met a lot of Tu-
pacs over the five years I covered him. All were complex, all
were thoughtful, and all were exhaustingly contradictory.

The last time we'd spoken at any length was shortly after
he'd been released from prison, where he'd spent nine
months for sexual assault. Here was the world-weary version of Tupac, the one who felt he'd been betrayed by some
of his closest friends and couldn't or wouldn't trust anyone
again. Given his circumstances during the previous twelve
months, I couldn't very well blame him. But the sight of him
that day caused me to recall the first time I'd met him, as a
fresh-faced, ready-to-tackle-the-world, aspiring movie star.

It was at the wrap party for the film *Juice* in New York City.
Tupac had the starring role of Bishop, an unstable high
school kid who wound up on a killing spree. His performance was haunting and amazing, and he completely up-
staged the other actors in the film. I was invited to the party
for background on the story I was doing on the director,
Ernest Dickerson, for the *Los Angeles Times*. Though I
vaguely remembered Tupac from his appearances in the
Digital Underground music videos, the videos did him little
justice. In person he was breathtaking. With his never-
ending, curly eyelashes, smooth mahogany skin, and a smile

that could reach the high heavens, Tupac's star potential was unquestionable.

We shook hands briefly as the publicist explained I'd be interviewing him the next day about his director. Over eggs and ham the next morning, we talked for hours about our favorite films. To my surprise, *Ordinary People* and *Terms of Endearment* were two films the then barely twenty-year-old knew well and liked. If you've seen these movies, you know they are two of the whitest, middle-of-America films you'll ever see on the big screen. Not a black person in sight for the entire two hours. But I loved them, and so did 'Pac. He broke down the plot lines of each (along with exact quotes) and why they touched him so much. I hadn't been covering hip-hop for long, but I knew this wasn't the normal exchange a rapper had with a reporter. He spoke excitedly about Shakespeare and other literary works that had influenced him when he was growing up. *Catcher in the Rye* and *To Kill a Mockingbird* were at the top of his list.

He also explained why he saw his music as an outlet for his political beliefs. Given his pedigree as the son of a Black Panther, it was only fitting that he would have a well-thought-out worldview. Still, the charm was all his own. Over the next few years, I'd run into him at various outings: parties for the show *In Living Color,* a Mary J. Blige concert, and sometimes even at the mall with a ton of friends, laughing it up as they bought jewelry and baggy jeans. Yet what I was seeing differed from what I was hearing about Tupac getting into fights with the who's who of black Hollywood. I heard the news of him being shot in a New York

City recording studio elevator a few months after I started at *Newsweek*.

Whereas two or three years previously I would have been surprised to hear about the rapper being the victim of bodily harm, the ever-changing Tupac had begun to take on a disturbing persona with his increasing wealth and fame. Most know the story of Tupac; he is indeed a legend at this point. However, it bears repeating that his childhood was a very complicated one.

Born to the Black Panther Afeni Shakur in June 1971, one month after she was acquitted on bombing charges, Tupac lived a somewhat nomadic life. His family shuffled between Harlem and the Bronx, and eventually landed in Baltimore. There he fell in love with all things cultural and entered the Baltimore School for the Arts, where he took acting and ballet. The family moved to Oakland, California, when he was in his early teens. He would later say this time was the beginning of a downward turn for him as he watched his mother start to use drugs and eventually moved out of the house to avoid seeing her waste away. He ended up on the streets selling crack to earn money, later hooking up with the rap group Digital Underground, working as their roadie. With time, his voice came to be heard on their records and his image featured in their music videos.

As Tupac's star rose, he often captivated American audiences with his unique lyrical style and timely commentary on injustices toward inner-city youth. It was ironic that the man who used his celebrity to speak about social injustice would end up time and again on the receiving end of violence and legal woes. The night Tupac was shot five times in

New York, the word got out quickly that rapper Christopher "Biggie" Wallace and Sean "P. Diddy" Combs were there as well. The suggestion that they were responsible wasn't made public at this point, so for the first few weeks most of the attention was focused on Tupac's injuries and his alleged whereabouts. The interest was heightened because the rapper was also then on trial for sexual assault.

Because of 'Pac's persona and ongoing run-ins with the law, *Newsweek* was particularly interested in what may or may not have happened that night in the studio. I spoke to different publicists and record company executives all day long, hoping for tidbits of information that might lead to my next move. Fortunately, I recalled one publicist had mentioned that Biggie was performing at the Apollo Theater that week. I needed to talk to him about Tupac, and calling his record company to ask for an interview wasn't going to work. So I devised Plan B. Early the morning after the shooting, I posted myself at the Apollo two hours before the rehearsal was to begin.

My intention was really just to ask Biggie what he'd seen, or not seen, heard or not heard, that night. At the time, I had no idea Tupac thought he and P. Diddy were behind the shooting, but I've always been struck by Biggie's unemotional responses when I approached him. Right on schedule, he drove up in a limo with his usual posse—Lil' Cease, D Rock, and a few others—in tow. I moved closer to the car as he emerged and politely stuck out my hand. "May I ask you a quick question, Mr. Wallace?" I explained that I was from *Newsweek* and that, although we'd never reviewed his music before, we would soon.

Biggie was caught off guard by my presence and totally unprepared to answer questions about a night I gathered he would have preferred to forget. But that's the job. He paused and looked me dead in the face as I asked him several times about where he was relative to Tupac that night in the studio. He made no effort to mask how annoyed he was. His answers were mostly "I don't remember" or "I didn't even see Tupac." Sensing I was going to get next to nothing from the rapper, I wrapped things up, but not before he added that he was sorry Tupac had gotten hurt but there was nothing he or Diddy could have done to prevent it. He seemed genuine as he made the remark. I'm not sure if anyone really ever understood the friendship Tupac and Biggie shared before the beef. I certainly didn't. I do know Biggie seemed to have a lot more to say than he did that morning.

Hitting a dead end in my research for a story that was perplexing both me and the New York Police Department, I decided to visit the hospital where Tupac had been taken the night before. I wasn't thinking I was going to talk to him in his hospital bed, but I did hope to find some of his friends, who might have a reason to speak out. There were police milling all around the hospital when I arrived, so I knew figuring out what floor the wounded rapper was on was going to be a chore. Thank goodness for employees who want to help a "sistah" out.

In a friendly exchange a male nurse's assistant let slip that Tupac was on the eighth floor. I made my way up with flowers in hand to avoid anyone thinking I was somewhere I shouldn't be. These are the times in this job when it really pays to be a black woman. People just assume you're with the group, or they don't give you much thought at all. When I got to the room, it was empty. Now I was really stumped. I didn't see many people anywhere on the floor. No police, and no friends or family there for other patients. This time, I cornered a female nurse's aide who happily reported that Tupac, her hero, had left the hospital against doctors' orders, just three hours after surgery had been completed.

This all added to the legend that Tupac was indestructible. He'd been shot just a day before and had major surgery to boot. Still, he rolled out of his hospital bed and kept moving to points unknown. Could the story get any deeper or more complicated? After working the phones for the rest of the day back at the office, I determined that he had settled into the home of Salt from the female hip-hop duo Salt-N-Pepa in Long Island.

For me, the discovery wasn't completely shocking, that is, Tupac ending up at a woman's home while so many people were looking for him all over the state of New York. 'Pac loved women, and women loved him. Some of my best leads during this time were from his loyal friends, like Jada Pinkett Smith and Jasmine Guy, who found it as hard to be his friend as it was just to walk away.

The very next week, Tupac was found not guilty of sodomy and weapons charges but guilty of sexual assault. The charges stemmed from the allegations of a twenty-one-year-old woman who said she was sodomized and sexually assaulted by Tupac and his friends in a New York City hotel room. I never thought the young man I talked to for hours about *Ordinary People* would end up in jail for assaulting a woman, but I never thought he'd die so violently either.

Tupac was sentenced to four and a half years in a maximum-security prison. It was while he was in prison that he implied to Kevin Powell of *Vibe* magazine that he felt P. Diddy and Biggie were behind his shooting. Although there was never any proof of their involvement, a war of not just words began.

While he was imprisoned, Tupac's albums continued to top the charts. His personality and plight fascinated many in the mainstream world and mesmerized young African Americans. His song "Dear Mama" became an instant cult anthem among inner-city youth. The most intriguing part of Tupac's prison time was that he didn't have to spend those nine months behind bars.

His lawyers were appealing the ruling, and he should have been free until the appeal was decided. But neither he nor his family nor his record label could or would post bail. A major recording star and lead in major films couldn't get up the money to stay on the outside? Most record executives knew of Tupac's many talents but were less than willing to take a chance on his volatility. At any point of his nine-month stay in prison, all someone would have had to do was post a million-dollar bond. All executives passed on the idea with the exception of one—Death Row Records CEO Suge Knight.

Knight had tried to snag Tupac for his label years before, when the rapper was on Interscope Records (Death Row's parent company), but 'Pac had turned him down, preferring to keep his own identity as an artist. But desperate times called for desperate actions, and Tupac knew he was hardly in a position to turn down help from anyone. Knight posted the $1.4 million bail in October 1995, and immediately Tupac signed with Death Row and flew to Los Angeles to begin recording *All Eyez on Me*.

Suge Knight certainly had a need for Tupac's services. His relationship with the heart and soul of Death Row—Dr. Dre—had gone downhill quickly and Snoop Dogg was on trial for murder. Tupac was, at that moment, the most talked about rapper on the planet. Knight had to have a part of him. This played right into Tupac's complicated ego. I remember getting the call from someone at the Death Row offices bragging about having Tupac on the label. They were in hog heaven about what it could do for the label's visibility— as if that was a problem—and what it would do for 'Pac.

With his in-your-face personality, Tupac rapidly became the center of all things Death Row. Artists who'd come before him at the label quickly faded from view in his presence. Suge Knight seemed to enjoy pitting his artists against one another. He felt it boosted their desire to be creative and productive for him. Tupac eagerly took the bait. He worked all night long on songs for *All Eyez on Me* and recorded like a madman until the album was completed. He actually didn't stop recording new material until shortly before his death, and we've seen the results in many new releases over the past decade.

Tupac took his visibility seriously, becoming a fixture at Snoop's trial, at Knight's turkey and Christmas drives in South Central, and at anything else that was related to Death Row. As Tupac and Knight became tighter, Knight's enemies became Tupac's, which only fueled the East Coast–West Coast rap wars. I watched as Dr. Dre carefully made his move to exit the company during this time. Attention was not something Dre enjoyed. Tupac's arrival at the company had put a not-so-positive spotlight on the business that didn't focus on the music, and Dre felt Death Row wouldn't survive. He was right.

It's still vivid, my waking up one Sunday morning and picking up the *New York Times* magazine section the way I do most weekends. On the cover, smiling from ear to ear, were Suge, Tupac, and Snoop under a headline that read, DO YOU KNOW WHO YOUR CHILDREN ARE LISTENING TO? It was incredibly sobering to see the three young men looking very sinister on the cover of one of the world's most important publications. It put "all eyez" not just on Tupac but on Death Row, and it would prove costly for all involved. By the year's end, Tupac Shakur would be dead and Suge Knight would be behind bars.

In the midst of the attention, Knight and Tupac continued to grow closer, spending outrageous sums of money on jewels, clothes, and women. Their friendship alienated many, but it seemed to give Tupac a sense of power. Knight was the protective big brother he'd never had, and he was reveling in it. But as both talked up the West Coast–East Coast battle between P. Diddy and Knight, even artists like Snoop Dogg politely backed away from the war of words.

With as much emphasis as he could muster during one interview two weeks before Tupac's death, a mellowed-out Snoop took pains to insist to me that he had no beef with anyone on the East or West side. "I just want to live to see my kids when I get home," he said. "I have problems with no one. I'm just doing my thing." Dre would echo that sentiment in numerous interviews during the bitter Death Row–Bad Boy feud.

What's not as easy to understand is when or if Tupac became disenchanted with Knight. Various sources have said he wanted to leave Death Row because he knew he'd signed a bum deal in order to get out of prison. Others suggest he was set to see a lawyer the week after he was shot to get his financial house in order. Indeed, upon his death, Tupac Shakur had less than $150,000 in the bank.

What I do remember is the last time I saw Tupac alive and well. It was at the after party for the MTV awards at New York's Bryant Park. Everyone was there, and 'Pac had changed from the gray suit he'd had on at the show to more casual attire. As usual, he traveled in a pack, so many people that you could barely see between the burly guys surrounding his small frame. He was seemingly happy, enjoying the massive attention he was getting from industry onlookers who had never seen him before.

My friend Trent wanted to walk over to meet Tupac, but I'd always been reluctant to approach the rapper in a crowd. Like it or not, Tupac attracted trouble like a magnet, and I had no plans to be around the next time it happened. Though we were staying at the same hotel in New York that night, I saw only Snoop and Nate Dogg trolling the lobby. Most of the glitterati crowd left on Friday morning for Las Vegas to attend the Mike Tyson fight while I stayed in New York to enjoy a prebirthday celebration on Saturday. I'd barely settled in for the night when I got a call from my editor telling me that Tupac had been shot and that I should get to Las Vegas as soon as possible.

I hopped the next plane and headed to the Flamingo, a hotel that directly faces the spot where Tupac had been shot. I knew Vegas pretty well since I'd attended many Mike Tyson fights there—or should I say hung out in the lobby at the fights, which was just as entertaining. After checking in, I rented a car and headed straight to the hospital where 'Pac was in critical condition. As I drove down the Vegas strip, I kept imagining how long he would've had to wait for an ambulance on a Saturday night. Las Vegas traffic is beyond a nightmare on any night, and during a fight night, you barely move an inch in an hour. For me, in little traffic, the hospital was more than a thirty-minute ride from the location of the shooting.

When I arrived, fans were all around the door holding up signs calling for Tupac's recovery. Inside the dreary building, more of 'Pac's friends milled the halls. Also there were Kidada Jones, Quincy Jones's daughter who was Tupac's girlfriend at the time, as well as the actress Jasmine Guy and other people I recognized but didn't know by name.

His mother, Afeni, and his aunt were standing guard near his door. At that point, I didn't know Afeni Shakur well, but I could tell by the anguish on her face that 'Pac wouldn't be leaving the hospital against doctors' orders this time. Standing there hoping to talk to one of his cousins, I had the opportunity to glance into his room. Tupac looked sound asleep, his bald head growing hair and his hand wrapped where two of his fingers had been shot off. He was taking long, labored breaths that made his entire body move up and down.

I looked away quickly when his aunt noticed me. I didn't want to intrude. For the next five days, I spent the mornings outside the hallway to Tupac's room. Security had buckled down, and we (the press) were getting pushed farther and farther away from the family. The following Friday, I was sitting outside with author and hip-hop journalist Kevin Powell when the news came that Tupac had died. I immediately went inside and cornered a nurse's aide to ask where the body was being taken. The aide didn't know the answer, but I believed him when he assured me that Tupac was indeed dead and that his body had been taken away as soon as it was pronounced to avoid unwanted pictures in tabloids. He would be cremated for the same reason.

For all his talk of death in interviews and in his music, one thing was obvious to me during the week I spent in that Vegas hospital. Tupac Shakur did want to live. He held on seven long days with severe injuries and massive blood loss, fighting to take every breath, and didn't give up until his body could give no more.

In the more than a decade since Tupac's death, I've had the opportunity to deal with Afeni Shakur many times. The pain which covered her face that day in the hospital hall is as apparent today as it was then. Though the legend of Tupac grows every year, the absence of a son never gets easier. What I admire most about his mother is her ability to own up to the part she played in her son's demise. She admits to being unavailable to him during a crucial time in his development and wonders what would have happened if they'd stayed in Baltimore. Such honesty takes a pride and strength that's beyond what any parent should have to summon up. But she is a unique woman, and he was an exceptional young man who left an undeniably unique legacy to a generation distinctly able to understand.

Bow Down
(to a Baller That's Greater Than You)

SHAQUILLE O'NEAL, KOBE BRYANT, AND
THE LOS ANGELES LAKERS

Shaquille O'Neal is in play mode. He's standing in the center of a warehouse on the north side of Orlando preparing to be photographed for a *Newsweek* article on the U.S. Olympic basketball team. It's 1996, and O'Neal is still the center with the Orlando Magic, so major funk with a certain teammate and a major NBA owner hasn't yet occurred. Fortunately, O'Neal is nowhere near the nightmare Orlando reps and some NBA sources predicted he would be when dealing with press. He doesn't complain about the extra time the photographer takes setting up a shot or the fiftieth question I ask regarding his career, his future, and what it was like to be the biggest kid throughout elementary school.

Instead, O'Neal playfully kicks the basketball to me as I struggle to write and kick back at the same time. This silly interaction would mark the beginning of my journey with Shaquille O'Neal, which has gone places I'm sure neither of us could have seen coming.

I hadn't been covering the NBA long when I met O'Neal that day in Florida, so his kindness stayed with me as what I'd hoped for each time out with a major sports star. But athletes are, in many ways, a captive audience for a reporter—they are required to talk to you after a game or a team practice, but they don't have to be nice about it. Trust me, many aren't.

Three months after my meeting with O'Neal, rumors that the gentle giant would be coming to Los Angeles to play with the Lakers started to spread like wildfire. It all made sense really, the Lakers were known for glitz, glamour, and winning, and lately none of those things had been happening. O'Neal had made a few films, a few rap albums, and he had a larger-than-life presence, precisely the kind of thing that sells tickets and exactly what the City of Angels is known for. A no-brainer.

At about the same time Los Angeles was bracing for the arrival of the storm known as Shaq, a sweet-faced Philly kid was packing his bags to come west as well. He'd enjoyed an amazing high school basketball career and gained even more attention for escorting the popular R & B singer Brandy to his high school prom. The son of a former NBA player, Kobe Bryant knew early on what he wanted from life. He grew up in Italy, from age three, with his two older sisters. By his sisters' own accounts, he was doted on endlessly by their parents. After moving back to the United States, the teenaged Bryant never fully fit in, partly because of his Italian roots and partly, one assumes, because of his Hummer-size ego, reportedly in full effect even in high school.

He was tall, handsome, and book savvy, and Bryant and his parents were intent on making the most of his many

talents. Although colleges around the country were climb-
ing all over him (he'd scored 1200 on his SAT), the NBA was
the only path Bryant was looking to stroll. After a showy
press conference announcing his decision to skip college for
the pros, he entered the 1996 draft as the thirteenth pick
overall and was taken by the Charlotte Hornets during the
first round.

However, for Bryant and his family, Charlotte would
never do. It was too south, too small, definitely not worthy
of the kid who'd patterned his game, his dress, and even his
speech after those of his idol, Michael Jordan. A well-
executed move by his parents and his agent got Bryant
traded to the ultrasexy Los Angeles Lakers within the week,
and the drama known as Kobe and Shaq began to unfold.

To say that I saw the supreme mess between these two
future legends coming would be less than honest. I already
knew of O'Neal's harmless but sometimes sensitive manner
and figured a boy right out of high school, playing in one of
the world's most glamorous cities, would just be in awe of
his surroundings for a while. Clearly, I'd never met Kobe
Bryant. The day I did meet him, I remember thinking what
an innocent-looking young man he was. You know the
phrase "deer caught in the headlights"? Well, that was Bryant. The eighteen-year-old's demeanor belied nothing of
what I later learned about him. In his rookie year, he was
the epitome of a well-mannered prep school kid, with his
clean-cut look, sans tattoos and visible bling, and his ear-
nest, straightforward way of answering any question you
posed to him. You had to love him.

From the preseason games around California, it was

abundantly clear that an international star was in the making. I immediately made plans for a big story in *Newsweek*. I approached Bryant with the idea while he was sitting on the sidelines watching a pickup game among his teammates. When I hinted that the story would suggest he was the next Jordan, a moniker I admit that's been applied to everyone from Harold Miner (Remember Baby Jordan? Where the hell is he?) to Grant Hill (Love Grant, but he's no Jordan), the kid from Philly nearly leaped out of his chair with excitement. This was his idol we were talking about, a man whose every movement Bryant had studied since the crib. In minutes, we'd made plans for me to meet his parents and talk to his friends, like the now Detroit Piston Richard Hamilton, to find out everything about Kobe Bryant. If only it had been that simple.

Had I been a little quicker in my thought process, I would have taken to heart what then Lakers coach Del Harris noted about Bryant those first few months of his rookie year. Sitting in the corporate offices of the Lakers in Inglewood, California, the coach spoke honestly about how he wished Bryant's handlers and advisers had let him begin his career in Charlotte. "This is not the place for a child," said Harris, stroking the all-white head of hair that made him look years older than he was. "I can't protect him in the locker room from those men who want to win now. They aren't trying to wait for him to learn. It's too much pressure."

I filed Harris's no-nonsense comments away until I met up with Kobe's dad, "Jellybean" Bryant, the next day. Jellybean, also known for his extreme confidence during his short and uneventful NBA career, dismissed the coach's remarks with a roll of his eyes and insisted his son was ready for anything. We'd met at the Santa Monica High School gym, where the younger Bryant liked to practice and play one-on-one with his dad. Watching Bryant interact with his father was pretty moving, given the much too often nonexistent relationship between fathers and sons in the NBA and, sadly, the African American community at large. The Bryant men seemed to have an unbreakable bond. In fact, so did the entire family, so much so that they all lived in a big house Bryant bought with his Lakers signing bonus. Every game ensured the attendance of Bryant's mother, father, and two sisters, cheering him on no matter what.

A rarely discussed fact in this soap opera is that Shaquille O'Neal was no stranger to having difficult teammates. Anfernee Hardaway had been no ray of sunshine down in Orlando, and O'Neal couldn't wait to get out of there. O'Neal wanted a team he could lead by himself, where he could use his supersize skills to win a few championship rings. He'd been given the impression the Lakers fit the bill. He clearly hadn't met Kobe Bryant either.

For a while all was good and quiet in Lakers land. It's hard to describe the vibe at the Forum and later the Staples Center during the heyday of Kobe and Shaq. I spent many a night attending games, whether I was working on stories or not, just to feel the electricity the players produced once they hit the floor. Their introductions were priceless, usually to the thumping beats of Ice Cube, Dr. Dre, or Snoop Dogg, which gave the team a larger-than-life Hollywood rollout. And, in fairness, it wasn't just the two marquee players who kept things interesting on the hardwood. Derek

Fisher, Rick Fox, and Robert Horry (along with a few others) all gave the Lakers a lot of the heart and soul the team exhibited in its best days. Fisher, Fox, and Horry were also invaluable measuring sticks of the Lakers' psyche once the locker room doors closed.

Not being a beat reporter, I didn't have the pressure of writing a story every night or the tedious job of describing each play during a game. Instead my stories tended to focus on personalities, lifestyles, and off-the-court actions. To do that, I had to develop relationships with the players who knew the real deal and didn't mind sharing it with a select few. It was indeed a few of those guys who gave early hints of the rapidly unraveling relationship between the two stars of the team.

The first season ended painfully, with Bryant taking several ill-advised shots against Utah that sent the team home quite early. By the beginning of the second season, rumblings of an alleged fistfight between Shaq and Kobe had leaked out. I chose not to harp too much on this revelation, even when I profiled Bryant during the first few months of the season. Instead I focused on his teen idol qualities and his tougher-than-nails confidence. I was still in denial. Yet my ears perked up when I heard several players discussing at length the way Bryant kept his distance from others on the team. They listed his penchant for dressing away from his teammates, his refusal to join them on postgame trips to clubs and parties, and above all, his extreme reluctance to pass the ball during games. Just one of these things was reason for concern, but the combination was a sign of a potentially ugly train wreck.

One snowy day in December 1997, I accompanied the team to Denver for a game against the Nuggets and hooked up with Bryant for a chat. We met by a fireplace in the hotel lobby for what had turned out to be my annual story on the baller. The rumors of Bryant's overworked ego were heating up, and I could no longer bury my head in the sand about the cute kid from Philly. On my way to meet Bryant that morning, I ran into O'Neal on the hotel elevator. We played our now typical game of who said what about him, true or not. He had a bevy of famous actress friends (this was before his marriage), and he knew I spoke to them regularly. The gentle giant loved to quiz me on who was doing what with whom and, of course, what they'd said about him. I won't name names, but rest assured the names were those of some of the most beautiful women in the business. After playing along for about ten minutes too long (I could never tell O'Neal I was meeting Bryant, as he would have felt it was a betrayal of sorts), I rushed to the lobby, hoping Bryant might be just a few minutes behind as well. He wasn't.

Dressed in a Lakers-issue gray hooded sweatshirt, sweatpants, and sneakers, Bryant smiled ever so sweetly while I made my apologies for making him wait. As I fumbled in my purse for my tape recorder, my mind raced with thoughts of how to navigate this conversation. I had to find a way to ask why so many of his teammates and players throughout the NBA had such a negative view of him. I pondered whether I should mention a trip I'd taken to Canada the previous summer. I'd gone at the invitation of another Lakers player, who was taking part in a Vince Carter charity game that was focused on raising money for underprivileged children and featured some of the most notable players in the league. I often attended events like this in the hope of getting to know some of the guys away from the pressures of NBA games and officials.

Usually these appearances are not filled with drama—no Ron Artest running-into-the-stands moments to air repeatedly on ESPN, and this Sunday night would prove no different, with the exception of one incident. After the game, a group of players moved on to a nightclub to do whatever rich, tall, and mostly good-looking men do after hours. One player ventured onto the stage to perform an unplanned freestyle rap, and he added a pretty stunning refrain. "Fuck Kobe Bryant." I nearly jumped out of my chair when I heard other players around me echo the words with identical disgust and anger.

There was little with which I could compare this situation. There had been talk for years that Michael Jordan was considered too arrogant for his own good. Who could forget Magic Johnson's and Isiah Thomas's infamous downgrading of Jordan in the 1988 All-Star game? Yet nothing this direct and hateful had ever been reported.

The nightclub incident played in my mind again and again, and caused me to realize I'd been in denial about Bryant's personality. His reserved nature, which impressed so many—particularly mainstream Americans—from afar, was a sort of emotional disconnection from others his own age. He kept to himself, I believe, because he didn't know what to say, and when he did speak, he was unsure how to say it. What many took as intellectual thoughtfulness could just as easily have been emotional immaturity intensified by lack of social interaction.

Bryant's decision to skip college had stunted him in ways

his family and advisers never fully expected. When we talked, Bryant often referred to college as an opportunity to read more books. He never seemed fully to grasp that college was also a chance to expand horizons and, even more important, to grow up. While the eighteen-year-old butted heads with the likes of O'Neal, Ruben Patterson, and Karl Malone in the big leagues, his high school buddies such as Richard Hamilton were learning collegiate team play and winning NCAA championships in front of less demanding crowds.

Too stubborn to admit a mistake, Bryant never hinted at regret over not taking the traditional route. However, I do remember a conversation with him one day after Hamilton's big NCAA win. The Lakers guard had watched the finals dutifully and jumped at the chance to talk to me about it when I asked. "That's what Richard always wanted to do," said Bryant with the innocent excitement of a child. "I watched it, and I thought for a minute I would have beat him if I'd been on the other team. Richard knows that. That would have been fun." He might have wanted to say more, but he couldn't. I don't believe he had the words to articulate a moment of doubt. He quickly regained his composure and mentioned he'd called Hamilton to congratulate him that night.

Watching Bryant strut his stuff for eight seasons at the same time he was trying to find his way—or better yet make his way—was like watching a man-child in the Promised land. He possessed so many traits of a superstar—the talent, the looks, and the boy-next-door quality that could sell consumers anything and everything with just a smile. But something always seemed to be missing. My belief was that he didn't have the feel of an authentic black male. Being a black male in America is such an exact science. Society insists that, to be fully accepted, young black men have to dress, speak, and act a certain way. Bryant could walk the walk on the basketball court, but once off the court, with his tendency to write poetry and listen to the music of Alanis Morissette, he never really fit in.

Bryant's inner conflict between his on-the-court and off-the-court personas is, in my mind, what sparked the epic battle between him and O'Neal. O'Neal felt that some rules of the game were not to be broken, and they included respecting your elders. Bryant failed to embrace this rule the entire time he and O'Neal played together. But winning can mask a lot of ugly things. The heyday of the Lakers' time under Shaq and Kobe could rival any rock-star moment. The fans, the celebrities, and the just plain partyers made Lakers games the hottest ticket in town.

One of my favorite moments occurred when the Lakers won their first championship. I managed after the game to get to the back and watch the players take pictures with the championship trophy. Shaq and his family, Derek Fisher and his family, and, last, Kobe and his crew gleefully posed with the silver statue as tears streamed down their faces.

Along with his parents and sisters that night, Kobe had the companionship of a young lady named Vanessa Laine, who was dressed in a skintight black minidress and mile-high stiletto heels. A beautiful woman at a player's side is normal in this game. What was surprising was that this woman, still in high school at the time, would soon become Kobe's wife. Their bond was evident, as she held on to Kobe so tightly I thought she'd squeeze the air out of his body. As the lanky player moved effortlessly through the crowded halls of the stadium, he seemed like the luckiest man in the world, a young player whose mother, father, and sisters were with him the entire way. There was nothing to hint that this cute kid with the world at his feet would take a huge tumble from grace.

I can still vividly remember getting a call from a friend telling me that Kobe Bryant had been arrested in Colorado. I laughed so loudly that I'm sure my neighbors thought I had Chris Rock in my living room. No way had Kobe gotten into that much trouble. There was just no way a kid who rarely drank, hated hanging out at nightclubs, and never boasted the bevy of women most NBA players were rumored to keep could have done what he was accused of doing. On paper, Kobe Bryant was as clean as they came. But nothing is ever what it seems.

Slowly and surely, Bryant's personality quirks were coming back to haunt him. When the details regarding his arrest on charges of sexual assault and rape began to flow into the media, my thoughts immediately raced back to Bryant's early days in the league. Older players had constantly offered to show him the ropes, and not just of the game. There was a separate set of ropes for coping with life in the fast lane. But Bryant had turned them down. After all, what could they tell him? A lot it turns out.

The average person is kidding himself if he doesn't realize that nearly every NBA player, every famous athlete really, has had a similar event happen. They've all met women who see nothing but stars in their eyes when a team lands in a city for a game. Women who take off from work to post up at the hotel all day and night just to catch the eye of a player. But this rarely ends up in the paper. It also rarely ends with an arrest. The reason is very simple. Game peeps other game.

From my first days covering the NBA, I quickly learned the ways ballers protect themselves from people they deem out to "get them." Several players I knew kept expensive trinkets on them at all times to give to women they bedded once the "act" was over. One of my favorite NBA players quietly admitted to me that he buys Cartier diamond tennis bracelets in bulk and gives one to every woman with whom he has a one-night stand. He gets the women's addresses and phone numbers and passes them on to his bodyguard before the evenings get too serious. According to this player, he does this to make sure no woman he has dealt with ever feels used or mistreated. "Nothing is free—not even that," he told me with a grin, but he was completely serious. It sounds seedy, I know, but the world of entertainment and sports is anything but aboveboard, so if you want to survive, you have to know how.

Until the summer Kobe Bryant was arrested, I'd enjoyed every moment of covering the Lakers. I'd had great relationships with the players, management, and public relations department for the majority of the eight seasons I wrote about them. But it all changed when I began having to pen stories about the team's favorite son's unfortunate transgressions. It had always been quite clear to me the love and support the Lakers' front office afforded Bryant. He was their golden child, the one with the movie-star looks, an integrated posse, and a vocabulary that all in charge could understand. As a onetime star Lakers player explained to me, "They don't love nothing more than a brother who knows his subject-verb agreement. He can be a damn fool as long as he speaks good English."

O'Neal, by contrast, was the Lakers' problem child. He was independent of thought and not particularly interested in pleasing the powers that be. So management, big shock, put their support behind Bryant, which posed a problem for me working for a magazine that holds no punches when it comes to hard news. Basketball games were one thing, fights in the locker room were another, but getting arrested on rape charges? Kobe would get no mercy at *Newsweek*.

Needless to say, I was a bundle of nerves during the first few weeks of the story. The magazine had decided to do a cover story, and it would include the eight seasons I'd spent reporting on Bryant as well as his current troubles. This new development put my stomach in knots. He had always been extremely cooperative with me. From the day I met him during training camp, he'd never turned down a request for an interview, never barked at having a photo taken for the magazine or giving me quotes for other stories. Conveying in a cover story the complexity of his personality and his arrest wasn't going to be easy. In fact, it was going to be one of the hardest pieces I'd ever had to do.

My painful experience began with the first story I did following Bryant's arrest. There was limited information on how his lawyers would proceed with the case, so much of the story would rehash previous stories, thoughts, and incidents. One person I spoke to regularly about Bryant was his fellow player and actor Rick Fox. Fox always provided a wealth of background information when I was writing stories about the team. His honest and straightforward way of describing people and events was neither mean-spirited nor envious.

For most of the years I'd spoken to him about Bryant's ups and downs, Fox had given me essentially the same quote. "Kobe is definitely a hard person to get to know, and because of that, we [the team] had left him on that island by himself—which was wrong." For the story I wrote just weeks after Bryant was indicted, I used Fox's quote again to explain a common perspective on the mess in which Bryant now found himself. The use of the quote infuriated the Lakers in a way that made it seem as if I'd personally made up the allegations against Bryant rather than reported on them. I guess they wanted a united front from the team in the wake of Bryant's arrest, but the reactions to the story and to me were beyond believable.

Not that I hadn't had my run-ins with the league and its teams before. The National Basketball Association can be a pretty sensitive organization, despite its size and reputation. Any negative reporting on the operation of a team or the lives and goings-on of the players would surely get a frown from the higher-ups. From Allen Iverson's ill-fated rap career to the players' union and the strike in the nineties, I'd had my share of friction with the league. The White House isn't known to love everything *Newsweek* or any other major publication writes. Nor does any public, visible organization made up of complex personalities and a plethora of

scandals and controversies. Why the NBA felt its circumstances would be different, I'm not sure.

Still, I was surprised that the Lakers took such a defiant
attitude toward me. As I began to report the cover story on
Bryant that was set to run about the time the trial opened, I
asked to attend the Lakers' training camp in Hawaii. Being
there would give me a good idea of the climate surrounding
Bryant and how his teammates really felt about yet another
major drama in his life. The first dilemma involved the unfortunate split between Bryant and his parents over his marriage to Vanessa Laine. While his parents and sisters had
been constant sources of support throughout Bryant's time
at the Lakers, the moment he married, his family seemed to
disappear from his side. It was a bad omen.

My request for a media pass was denied by the Lakers
PR rep John Black, who cited the Rick Fox quote as the
reason. After eight seasons of my covering the team and
numerous articles by other reporters that were deemed "unfair" or wrong, I'd been singled out by the same PR person
who often chastised me about writing so many hip-hop stories in *Newsweek*. I had mostly laughed off these comments. Now, with his refusing me access in order to do my
job, I no longer took his dismissive attitude toward hip-hop
culture so lightly.

In reality, the Lakers couldn't prevent me from coming
to training camp. *Newsweek*'s lawyers had the right and the
ability to fight the team's refusal, but I was less than enthu-
siastic about using that option. Plus, I had a cover story to
write, and my focus was on trying to make it as fair as I
could. Putting an African American male on the cover of a

mainstream publication for being arrested was something I couldn't take lightly. The story needed to be balanced, nuanced, and above all to represent an accurate account of the events leading up to what allegedly occurred in that hotel room. It wouldn't be about whether Bryant did it or not, because there was no way to write that story before the facts were presented at trial, but it would outline what ill-advised decisions had brought him to that point.

At the end of editing the eight-page story, I was offered a byline on the cover by the top editor. It was an honor that I'd never before been offered, but I turned it down because of my conflicting emotions about the subject. As I expected, the article got massive coverage. I did many of the television and radio shows, mostly clarifying my thoughts on Bryant as a person. Katie Couric and Larry King both asked if I thought Kobe was guilty. All I could say was it wasn't my impression of the man, but rape is never something you can guess about. Still, it was important for me to be true to the young man I'd dealt with on so many occasions and with whom I'd frequently had very positive experiences.

Of course, the Lakers were not pleased with the story and based on subsequent television show appearance cancellations, I could not help but think it was a direct result of the Lakers' displeasure with my story. A popular ESPN commentator who is a huge supporter of the Lakers and Bryant, went so far as to tell Larry King about the Lakers' displeasure with my first story. I was in total disbelief that another journalist—who'd never met me and never asked how I'd come about my story—would repeat such gossip.

I often think this would not have happened to a white

male sports journalist, accustomed as they are to having their say about black athletes without long-term repercussions. But to have someone other than the status quo, particularly someone who was not a sports beat reporter, weigh in just wasn't acceptable. To prove my suspicion, sports newscaster Jim Gray, another huge supporter of Bryant, only weeks before the season began, reported several degrading remarks by Bryant regarding O'Neal's "childlike selfishness and jealousy" and questioning his leadership and his physical preparedness. As expected, the remarks received a lot of media attention. Whether intentional or not, they paved the way for Shaq's very public departure from Los Angeles.

Nearly three years later, Kobe Bryant is moving toward redeeming himself with appearances at inner-city schools and in advertisements that try to dig deep into his psyche. During the aftermath of Hurricane Katrina, Bryant was the first to volunteer to play in a charity game for the victims, and now he works at developing friendships with other players.

But while mainstream America might be back onboard with Bryant, gaining the favor of African Americans at large is quite another matter. Before his arrest, Bryant had a rather shaky relationship with the African American community, mostly because of his perceived disconnect from the culture. He would later explain in a *Dime* magazine feature, "Because I grew up in Italy, I felt I didn't have the right to go into the inner city and preach to those kids." While this perspective was insightful, Bryant failed to realize that having grown up in the 'hood is not the only basis on which a player can relate to his community.

In 2006 against the Toronto Raptors, Bryant put in an eighty-one-point game, the second highest total in NBA history, which will definitely make him one of the greatest players ever. To cap off what has been a phenomenal season, he led the Lakers to the 2006 playoffs, in part because of the return of Coach Phil Jackson and the superstar's realization that eighty-one points alone would not redeem him in a town that felt he had contributed to the premature end of a winning dynasty. He would need to prove he could get another championship ring without Shaquille O'Neal. With his extensive ESPN *SportsCenter* highlight reel, Bryant was a front-runner for last season's MVP title. And he's gotten Nike back on his side.

Yet the court of public opinion is still out on Bryant. On the one hand, he placed fifth on the Ten Most Hated Athletes list in *GQ* magazine's February 2006 issue and still faces a sea of boos, rather than applause, when he enters certain arenas around the country. On the other hand, there were the popular Nike "Love Me or Hate Me" television ads featuring Bryant's Zoom Kobe 1 shoe, and it's been reported that sales of his Lakers jersey are soaring, placing it in the top five in the NBA.

Despite the wildly popular Number 8 jersey, in a somewhat baffling move (he is baffling no matter how many points he scores), Bryant requested that his jersey number be changed for the 2006–7 season to 24, the number he wore at the start of his high school basketball career in Ardmore, Pennsylvania. Some in the sports world feel this is the superstar's attempt to rid himself of the painful past associated with Number 8. Kobe Bryant seems to be on the fast track back to the top, but the climb back up is never quite as easy—or as rapid—as the fall.

In an ironic twist, only a year after leaving the Los Angeles Lakers and joining the Miami Heat, center Shaquille O'Neal won his fourth NBA championship. This was a tough pill to swallow for die-hard Los Angeles Lakers fans who felt O'Neal's departure from the team was one of the biggest upsets in franchise history. I suspect that for O'Neal, winning again without Bryant, Buss, and Jackson was a vindication of sorts. Interviews I had with O'Neal the year after he left Los Angeles made it clear that he was hurt by the way things ended and that only another championship could ease the sting of disappointment.

In Miami, O'Neal had found another great player in Dwyane Wade, and the combination of the two players would prove to be dynamic. Wade was, for lack of a better analogy, the anti-Kobe. Humble, secure, and with dirt-poor origins, Wade seemed happy just to be in a position where he could live a better life. "I've never played with a better player than Dwyane," said O'Neal. "He's the best, and I'm not just talking about his skills on the court. That's only half of it. I'm talking about as a person—a person who understands how to get along and deal with others and share. We've been on the whole page from the day I got here. In fact, I called him before I came and broke it down for him so he'd know what was and wasn't true about L.A." O'Neal went on to add that he felt Wade's college education helped tremendously in his development as a player and a person.

To be honest, I was pleased that O'Neal got a chance to win one more championship. In all my years of covering the league, I've never had more enjoyable interviews or covered a personality who was as admired and respected by his peers. It was also meaningful to see him win because he is truly the last of a generation in the NBA, a generational bridge, which after Michael Jordan, clears the way for the Lebrons, Dwyanes, and Carmellos. While, at thirty-four years of age, O'Neal's best years might be behind him, I doubt there is another player on the horizon who'll be able to match O'Neal's charisma, style, and monster skills anytime soon.

And the Oscar Goes to . . .

ANGELA BASSETT AND WHOOPI GOLDBERG

One of the more difficult aspects of being a black journalist, in my opinion, is the huge responsibility you face each time you're enlisted to cover an African American subject for a mainstream publication. To complicate matters, there is also the general, unsolicited familiarity that sometimes arises with subjects, which can lead to comments being made on the record, by both the reporter and the person being interviewed, that may cause unintended controversy. Although I admit, I interviewed Tom Hanks once, and he seemed pretty familiar, too. But I digress.

I've encountered the familiarity situation many times while on interviews for *Newsweek,* and for the most part, it proved to be a very beneficial tool for me. I think it was equally advantageous for the person I was interviewing, in the sense that the more familiar the subject, the better the interview, which means the reader gets a truer picture. Sometimes, however, that familiarity can cause unforeseen problems. Never before had this been more evident to me than in my interview with the Academy Award–nominated actress Angela Bassett in 2002.

Marvet Britto, a well-connected New York publicist and friend, represented Bassett during this period and offered me a chance to write a piece about how Hollywood had ignored the immense talent of this Yale-educated actress. The story was right up my alley given the success of my profile of Denzel Washington, as well as previous stories I'd penned about the plight of black actresses in Hollywood. Bassett was an excellent example given her amazing performances in movies such as *What's Love Got to Do with It?* and *Malcolm X*. Her regal cheekbones and flawless brown complexion, although stunning, made her sort of an "everywoman," and the apparent lack of acknowledgment of her immense talent deserved an extensive reported piece. What would make this feature all the more interesting—and timely—was the fact that Halle Berry had won the Best Actress Oscar a few months before. I think many in the industry and the African American community at large had quietly expected Bassett to be the first out of the present generation of actresses to win the coveted statue. I know I did.

With my focus clear, we set the interview up for a Friday afternoon at the Four Seasons Hotel in Beverly Hills, the same hotel where I'd interviewed Denzel, for good karma. I arrived early to get myself situated and to prepare my tapes and questions. Bassett arrived about fifteen minutes later, looking breathtaking. Her skin glowed, her hair was in a modified, honey-hued, curly Afro, and her fit, muscular frame was highlighted by the beige tank top she was sporting. As usual, I softballed a few questions to begin with, asking about her background, childhood, family, and education. Much of this I already knew, but you never know when a celebrity is going to decide to release some new introspective observation.

Slowly, as Bassett became more comfortable, we tackled the issue of inequality in Hollywood and how it affected her life and career. She candidly spoke about how, after getting an Oscar nomination for *What's Love Got to Do with It?*, she sat by the phone for months, waiting for work to come her way again. "But I didn't work again for another year and a half. I guess I was pretty naïve to think it would be different, that it was just about the talent, particularly for someone who looks like me. You forget that sometimes." This was both astounding and distressing to hear. I, of course, realized that there were few opportunities for minority actresses, but Bassett had been at the head of the class for so long, it was hard to imagine her sitting idle, without an audition.

Bassett went on to recall missed opportunities to work with the legendary Sean Connery and other notable mainstream actors. "Sean told me he would love what our being in the film would mean across the board for black and white," she revealed. "I remember him saying how beautiful our skin would look next to each other's, and how I was perfect. I left the meeting thinking, 'It's mine.' But a few weeks later, they cast a lesser-known actress at the time" (Catherine Zeta-Jones). Bassett continued to walk down memory lane, recounting how she was often just about to get the role, but politics, or some other glitch, got in the way.

From there, it seemed only natural that the conversation turned toward *Monster's Ball,* the film for which Halle Berry recently won an Oscar. It was rumored that Bassett was offered the role before Berry but passed on it. Bassett confirmed this chain of events and talked extensively about how much she disliked the story line and the way it was executed. The plot revolves around a young southern woman with a husband on death row and a young, obese son at whom she often directs her frustrations and anger.

The character also begins a somewhat seedy relationship with a male security guard at the prison. The relationship ends in a torrid, graphic love scene with a partially nude Berry. Bassett challenged the mother's treatment of the boy and various other subplots she deemed unrealistic and contradictory. The actress said she had this discussion with the producers of the film and felt her criticisms probably weren't appreciated very much.

Our talk then turned toward the obvious. Had Berry's Oscar win made Bassett regret turning the role down? Bassett paused for a second and then answered with a firm no. The next comment—without a doubt—caused both of us a great many sleepless nights: "I wasn't going to be a prostitute on film," she told me. "I couldn't do that because it's such a stereotype about black women and sexuality. . . . Film is forever. It's about putting something out there you can be proud of ten years later. . . . Meryl Streep won Oscars without all that." It was truly a quote heard around the world.

At the moment the words came out of Bassett's mouth, I knew they would get attention. I mean, she was criticizing Hollywood for the unfortunate rules African American women had to play by. She was saying what so many black actresses wanted to say, needed to say, but couldn't. Bassett would later find out why.

Still, we continued to talk about things in general. Dates from hell, her mother's old boyfriends, and the ins and outs of married life. It was a pleasant, "girly-girly" connection which yielded the type of information that could jump-start any decent biography down the road. The interview officially lasted five hours, one of the longest I've ever had. In fact, by the end I had no tapes left to record or notebooks to write in.

Bassett said many hot-button things during those hours—not mean-spirited in context, but words that could certainly have been interpreted as sour grapes and with malicious intent toward others. But none of the interpretations were true. I was there with her in that moment and saw the pain of a fragile woman who'd had expectations and, in some ways, promises of a better career and life that had not come to fruition. It was an all too familiar look, and one that was hard to explain within the confines of a two-page news story.

These were also thoughts that she couldn't share with her peers for fear of harsh judgment or with a random associate who might question the validity of her assumptions. Instead she'd shared them with me. I often wished she hadn't. The completed piece was one I was extremely proud of. It carefully arched the highs and pitfalls of an amazing actress's résumé. The *response* to the piece, however, was something I couldn't have predicted in a million years. Lost was the story of a woman whose career had stalled for no reason.

Within hours of the story's release, media outlets zeroed in on that one quote, and they didn't let go for weeks. It's also important to note what didn't get highlighted. I'd written, "Bassett is clear she isn't criticizing Berry—just the way Hollywood views women in general and black women in particular," as well as quoted Bassett, "I can't and don't begrudge Halle her success. . . . It wasn't the role for me, but I told her she'd win . . . and to go get what was hers." Despite those clear, positive messages from Bassett about Berry, the perceived negative comments stood alone. People who hadn't read the story accepted what they heard, and a cruel media storm descended upon Bassett.

I sank every time I saw Angela Bassett's name dragged through the mud in print or her pained expression on the red carpet when she was asked if she had hard feelings toward Berry. Bassett eventually backed away from that quote, indicating she had never said those words. I wasn't surprised at this, though many thought I'd be mortified. I would have done the same thing in her position, as most celebrities do when the heat gets fiery hot.

I do question regularly what would have happened if I'd left that one quote out of the story, what heartache it would have saved Bassett and possibly Berry, who never publicly responded. I also wonder about a society that doesn't allow people to express their opinions without fear of backlash. Bassett wasn't the only African American who had issues with the graphic nature of *Monster's Ball*. I'd written numerous stories with much more salacious content that had simply disappeared into nowhere. Who could have known?

I've seen Bassett a number of times since the story appeared, and I wanted to run at each occasion. She's pleasant to me because she's too professional not to be, but I'm sure she cringes at the thought of how a moment of honesty had gone so wrong. That makes two of us.

The experience with Angela Bassett made me a bit gun-shy for several months. Nonetheless, I jumped at the chance to interview Whoopi Goldberg the moment I realized she would be returning to Broadway in the Pulitzer Prize–winning playwright August Wilson's *Ma Rainey's Black Bottom*.

We'd met in 1997, when she released her bestselling book titled simply *Book*. We did our interview on the rather luxe train car that she owned and had attached to a cross-country Amtrak train. Goldberg didn't mind flying, but she preferred the safety of a train car when not in a hurry. I flew to Kansas City to meet up with the train and rode from there to Los Angeles over the course of two days. The train car was not very different from an apartment, with a couple of bedrooms, a private bath, a fully equipped kitchen, and a private chef. The surroundings also reminded me of my grandmother's parlor in that Goldberg had personal effects like blankets, lamps, and family photos scattered about.

My past, very honest chats with Goldberg were fond memories for me, but I was totally blindsided by our interview in New York in early 2003. Before our meeting, somewhere between Santa Fe and Nevada, I didn't know what to think of Goldberg. I'd never gotten over the early nineties, when her considerable talent was eclipsed by her relationship with the actor Ted Danson. Not that I disregarded her grand entrance into the limelight with her role in *The Color Purple*, or the groundbreaking stand-up routine she per-

formed, featuring the infamous bit about being a white girl
with long, blond hair, which she aptly demonstrated by putting a white towel on her head and swinging it back and
forth. That bit was masterful, but it wasn't what made me
want to know more about the woman born Caryn Johnson.

Her ill-fated relationship with Danson was more than
mind-boggling to me, and not just because she is black and
he is white. Their racial divide proved to be only the back-
drop to Danson's much talked about appearance in black-
face at a roast honoring Goldberg at the Friars Club in New
York in October 1993. The resulting blowup lasted for several months and seemed to make the usually unflappable
Goldberg quite defensive. This only made her much more
interesting to me, but it would be years before I'd get the
chance to meet her face-to-face.

When I did meet her, I found her to be a very likable
woman, one whose confidence on film and onstage masked
a certain insecurity she let only a few people see. We talked
for an hour or so about her book, which was funny in a way
only Whoopi could be. She feared no one on those pages,
and few subjects were left unturned. But the real conversation occurred when the tape was turned off and we discussed the days when her name got films made and her
performances won Oscars.

Goldberg hadn't experienced a lot of the woes of many
other African American actresses of her generation, such
as working in endless low-budget films before getting noticed, and she seemed grateful for that. She was actually
embraced by the Hollywood honchos from the moment
Quincy Jones and Steven Spielberg announced her as the

next big thing during the eighties. Before being discovered, Goldberg had struggled with growing up dirt poor in public housing in New York City and later surviving as a single mother on welfare.

But those obstacles were nothing compared with her internal battle. With deep mahogany skin, kinky hair, and other strong African features, Goldberg felt the sting of not being considered pretty enough from the moment she was able to understand what beauty is and how it can be used to get ahead. I had always been aware that her skin tone and other African features were not the ideals of beauty in the African American community. So it makes sense that Goldberg would build a wall around her feelings on these issues. She dealt by telling jokes, and that defense became her ticket to a better life. By the time she made it to Hollywood, the mainstream was so enamored by Goldberg's unique style that she shot to stardom before she had time to put it all in perspective. When she did, however, she realized that many African Americans were still punishing her for something she could do nothing about. Her looks.

During our train ride across the West, Goldberg discussed at length her frustrations with the community's idea of beauty and with comedians such as the onetime late-night talk show king Arsenio Hall, who constantly made crude jokes about her tendency to date white men. "They do it all the time, but when I do, it's an issue," said Goldberg about a number of African American male celebrities. "Those men who make the comments weren't asking me out. So who do they suggest I date?"

I was taken aback for a moment by her brutal honesty

and her obvious feelings of rejection from her own people. Our talk on the train that day reminded me of her winning an NAACP Image Award for Outstanding Actress in a Motion Picture in 1992 for the film *Ghost*. She accepted the award with words that made it clear she hadn't felt the love from the black community before that day. But as forthright as Goldberg was during our train trip, she would be even more so in a dank theater dressing room on a rainy Thursday afternoon some five years later.

I arrived early to get a chance to watch her photo shoot for the magazine. She was in true Whoopi mode, telling jokes, puffing on a cigar, and refusing any overly girly makeup and hair attention from the camera crew. Seeing that all was well with the shoot, I moved upstairs to her dressing room and remember fondly passing the late, celebrated playwright August Wilson and the late Tony Award–winning director Lloyd Richards chatting excitedly outside her door. As on her train, Goldberg's room was filled with memories and trinkets from her home and a video camera set up so she could see and talk to her grandchildren living in California. She soon greeted me with a warm hug, surprisingly remembering our long-ago talk. Though it shouldn't have been a surprise at all, she signed my copy of her book that day with the inscription, "To Allison: For the things we both know."

After discussing why she'd returned to Broadway and how this time differed from her stint there some twenty years before, I felt I needed a little more variety in the piece, so I probed her feelings about hosting the Academy Awards just the year before. She'd been the mistress of ceremonies

on the historic night that both Denzel Washington and
Halle Berry won. I asked the question thinking she'd give a
pleasant answer about what a special night it had been and
how she was grateful to have been a part of it.

"I'm glad Denzel won," said Goldberg with a straight
face and without flinching a muscle. I just froze. Not again,
I thought. I cannot go there. I mean, hadn't she read what
Angela Bassett said and what she went through after she
said it? Didn't she know that I'd wanted to crawl under a
rock for a month after receiving angry letters from African
Americans criticizing me for airing the community's dirty
laundry? I guess not.

I'd opened the door to a line of questioning about a topic
that Goldberg was more than eager not to just walk but to
run through. The fact that she had hosted the Oscars wasn't
the only event of significance. She was also one of the
two—and the only living—black actresses who'd won an
Oscar in the past. Goldberg won a Best Supporting Actress
award for *Ghost* in 1991.

Yet Berry's tear-filled acceptance speech did not ac-
knowledge Goldberg or Hattie McDaniel, the first African
American to win an Oscar, at all. Goldberg was royally insulted by this slight, and when I mentioned that perhaps
Berry forgot in her moment of joy, the comic responded,
"She looked at my black face the entire night. How could
she forget? . . . You figure, if she's not going to recognize
me, why should anyone else?" She added: "And if she did
forget, why haven't I heard from her? Why didn't she call or
write to say she forgot?"

It was hard to disagree about the speech Berry made,

which included thanks to the actress Vivica A. Fox yet not to one of the women who'd come before. Goldberg's words were direct and sharp, but I again realized that these were the thoughts of a woman who'd been publicly ignored at a historic moment and wanted others to feel her pain. We continued to chat about her disconnect with many other African American actresses and about her self-proclaimed "outsider" status. Yet she didn't seem to mind being on the outside looking in. She was used to it.

Goldberg also touched on how she'd hoped to make a difference. In fact, her words seemed eerily similar to those of Bassett when it came to her status as an actress in Hollywood. "I'm not sexy enough for those in power, and that limits the stuff I get considered for. I'd hoped early on to change that image of what made a woman sexy, particularly a black woman. I really thought my looks would say that it's okay to just be who you are and look the way you look, but nobody wanted to listen."

A modified version of our interview ran in the magazine the same week the space shuttle *Columbia* exploded as it descended over Texas, killing all aboard. Goldberg's harsh comments about Berry got lost in the aftermath of that tragedy, and I can't say I'm regretful. You might ask, why would I publish information that I knew would cause a storm, especially after the Angela Bassett fiasco? The answer for me was simple. Because that was what Whoopi Goldberg said and what she meant. In fact, her words said just as much about her as they did about Berry, and readers needed to know. Further, I felt confident that Goldberg could and would stand behind her comments and would not be browbeat by either the public or the press into taking it back. Bassett was polite and fragile, Goldberg was neither.

I still look forward to my interviews with Whoopi Goldberg whenever they occur. The clarity with which she sees Hollywood and her place in it creates a discussion that changes each time we meet. Goldberg is the devil's advocate by default in an industry that likes sameness in every aspect of the game. She doesn't play by those rules, and she's paid the price for it. You have to admire her resilience.

Sexiest Man Alive

Denzel Washington

P lease let this fine man be late, too!" Those were the words swirling in my head as I sat stuck in traffic on Rodeo Drive in Beverly Hills one November day in 1999. I had taken an ill-advised shortcut, hoping to save time by avoiding major streets in order to get to the Four Seasons Hotel during rush hour. What was I thinking? It's always rush hour in Los Angeles. I had an interview at four o'clock, and I was running a good twenty minutes late. You'd think I'd have known by now that everywhere in Los Angeles is thirty minutes away, even if you're right across the street. But I'd gotten held up on a phone call with someone who had no idea how important the day was for me. I had an interview, and it wasn't with just anyone, not just any star, not just any actor. I had an interview with Denzel. No last name necessary.

Just the sound of his name sends chills down the spine of pretty much any woman alive, so it doesn't take much to imagine what seeing him in the flesh would do to a woman such as myself. Boy, was I nervous, and in truth, it didn't fully make sense. It wasn't like I hadn't met him before. I'd interviewed him while I was an intern at *Newsday* in New York. But that had been more than ten years—a lifetime, another era—ago. Before he was the Denzel with an Oscar and a *People* magazine "Sexiest Man Alive" cover. I'm sure any black woman over thirty years of age can tell you how much and how long she's loved Denzel Washington. But my story is quite different, and I take pride in boasting to anyone just how early my love affair with Dark Gable began.

As the only child of an elementary school teacher, I was encouraged to read books more than watch TV. The popular shows of the day were not often on in my house, and when the television was on, it was usually tuned to *60 Minutes* or some other drab news show. Periodically, I'd get to watch scandalous soap opera–type dramas like *Knots Landing*, and on Saturdays, you'd have to kill me to make me miss an episode of *Fantasy Island*.

But during the week, I stuck to my homework and magazines and to nonstop telephone gabfests with my girlfriends, Dollie and Carlotta. Those facts make it sort of hard for me to remember exactly how I happened to tune in to an episode of the ultra-adult, ultraserious medical drama *St. Elsewhere*. The show was brilliant in every way, but not exactly the stuff junior high school students just had to watch. Not only did it come on at 10:00 P.M. (very late for a school night), but it featured story lines like rape, suicide, and murder, in dream sequences no less. A real downer. But something about that show made me a fan from the moment I saw it, and by the second episode, I had seen perhaps the finest black man with the thickest thighs (he sometimes wore shorts on the show) and the most noble walk ever to hit prime time. Denzel. Until that point, Todd Bridges had been the cutest man-child on television to me. How sad is that?

For years after that fateful night, I talked to my high school buddies about this man named Denzel. They knew nothing of him, never saw the show or heard about him as an actor (who really saw him in *Carbon Copy*?). While my friends swooned over the little rough-around-the-edges boys in the R & B group New Edition, I kept on watching my ten o'clock show to see what a real man looked like. And then it happened. *A Soldier's Story* hit movie theaters in 1984, and I about died to go see it. I hitched a ride with friends to the theater, and while they saw *Halloween 10* or something, I watched Denzel. Over and over, I watched the film. To date, I've seen *A Soldier's Story* about thirty times, five times in theaters. I have a good laugh when I think of the time I told Denzel about my multiple viewings of that movie, and saw his facial expression of true concern.

With the movie's moderate success, Denzel's name became more familiar, my crush was no longer exclusive. But I maintained that I was one of his truest fans. After my sophomore year in college, I headed to New York for a journalism internship in entertainment with *Newsday*. I was in the big leagues now, but they weren't exactly handing over the major stories on boldfaced names to interns. As it turned out, though, midway through the summer I found out that Denzel, a New York native with extensive background in theater, would be starring with Ruby Dee and Vanessa Williams in a play on Broadway called *Checkmates*.

Of course I immediately told my editor and begged for

the chance to interview the actor. In the mainstream world,
Denzel was not quite a star yet. In fact, I met him shortly
after he'd finished filming what would be his Oscar-winning
role in *Glory*. He was so unknown to the mainstream press
that I had no opposition from full-time reporters on securing the interview.

I remember the day of the interview as if it were yester-
day. I got my hair done, my teeth cleaned, and went to the
mall staple casual wear store The Limited to get the finest
clothes an intern making two hundred dollars a week could
buy. And that wasn't much. Now don't get me wrong. My
little shopping spree and beauty ritual was purely an innocent gesture. I was aware of the existence of a Mrs. Washington. Pauletta. In fact, that was what made Denzel even
more appealing. His wife was a regular, down-home sister
from the South, something a southern woman like myself
had to appreciate.

Our chat was to take place at the theater where the play
was being performed. I was extremely nervous, but I was
ready. The play's publicist took me to the actor's dressing
room and instructed me to wait until Mr. Washington came
back from lunch. About ten minutes later, the door swung
open, and the man, the myth, the legend walked in. I nearly
fainted. He was dressed in what I'd later learn is his trade-
mark uniform. Nothing special. A rumpled white T-shirt,
wrinkled jeans, and barely combed hair. I and thousands of
other women might have thought he was the cutest thing
ever, but he clearly didn't spend much time worrying about
that aspect of his appeal.

The beginning of the interview was nerve-racking, as

they tend to be. Denzel wasn't exactly garrulous, and I hadn't exactly perfected the art of the interview. Plus, I was fighting hard not to give away the fact that I was a measly intern. He looked me up and down. I'm sure I looked a hot mess, with my overironed beige linen pants, beige flat leather shoes, and Peter Pan collar shirt. I looked like I was going to a church social. It was so obvious that he asked me where I was from as soon as we sat down. When I told him Georgia, he said, "That makes sense, because you look wholesome." For some reason I was quite offended by the word *wholesome*. There can be a fine line between wholesome and backwoods country, and nobody, including Denzel, was going to insult me to my face. He laughed when I challenged the comment and said I just looked young and not from the big city. Was it that obvious?

He then offered to look *wholesome* up in the dictionary for me. I calmed down a bit since he seemed very concerned that he'd hurt my feelings. The comment was in fact just the icebreaker I needed, and we slowly moved into what turned out to be a great interview, the model for the interviews I've experienced with Denzel a dozen times since. Starting off slow, then moving fast forward at warp speed. Some of the earlier questions to which he'd given short, uninspired responses were brought up again and answered in great detail. We'd clicked. We must have talked for three hours, with some of that time being used to talk about me. Denzel wanted to know about *me*! Right. With his increasingly busy schedule and the number of people he encountered, I'm sure he forgot me the second I walked out of the door. But it had me floating the rest of the day.

Fast forward to November 1999. This time I'm interviewing the actor about *The Hurricane,* and his starring
role as the boxer Rubin "Hurricane" Carter, who was sent
to prison for crimes he said he didn't commit. I arrived at
the Four Seasons and literally jumped out of my still-moving
car to get to the lobby area. Denzel was nowhere to be
found. Had he left? Then his publicist, Alan Nierob, walked
in and told me the actor was running a bit late but was on
his way. Safe!

Walking through the lobby had been hard enough. Jodie
Foster was at one table, and Brad Pitt was at another. None,
of course, compared with Mr. Washington, who arrived in
typical I'm-so-the-man fashion. He hugged Foster and
mouthed "Hi" to Pitt before making his way to my table.
Since the last time we'd met, I'd worked at the *Los Angeles
Times,* written a children's book, and blown up plastic dinosaurs for Steven Spielberg. I was as calm as a cucumber. I
didn't ask if he remembered me because I so hate when
writers do that, even if they have met the subject a number
of times before.

We hit it off quickly this time, partly because we now
had mutual friends in the business. Throwing out familiar
names always gets the ball moving rapidly. This would turn
out to be my best Denzel interview. It lasted for well over
four hours, and we discussed everything from the mega-
house he was building to his father's death and the recent
deaths of his wife's parents, which had affected him deeply.

Unfortunately, little of that conversation made it into
the story I wrote for *Newsweek*. It's often hard to fit all the
information a subject tells you into a piece, particularly if it
has no direct relationship to the purpose of the story. This

can be one of the trickiest issues for a journalist, especially when you feel you've gotten a complicated subject like Denzel to dig really deep into his feelings. Washington's on-screen reserve is just as true of his offscreen persona. He takes his time to mull every question posed to ensure that his responses leave nothing to off-kilter interpretation.

It was touching to hear him discuss at length his oldest son's football aspirations and his daughter's parent-teacher meetings. He also spoke about his wife's close relationship with her siblings. "It doesn't matter what's going on—whether it's my son playing in a high school game or what—her brothers and sisters will all fly in to watch just to show support," he said. "They're a tight bunch like that, and I love it."

Another quality about Washington not usually written about is the reverence he has for higher education. He told me for the first time that he'd dropped out of college for a while. "I worked at the post office and picked up trash until I figured out I needed to get back into school," he said. His wife's father had been president of a historically black university, and Washington spoke of his father-in-law with absolute admiration. His wife's North Carolina pedigree, which was heavily centered on academics, seemed to give Washington comfort and pride.

Washington's own father had been a minister and provided the foundation for his strong faith as a young man and an adult. "I read my Bible every day without fail," said the actor. "It's something that's always been a part of my life, and it hasn't changed." He also described his frequent donations to his California church and how that money had helped build a new, larger sanctuary.

The next year *The Hurricane,* as did many of his films, garnered Washington a Best Actor Oscar nomination, and many felt he would win for sure this time. He'd lost to Al Pacino in 1993, despite his numbing portrayal of Malcolm X. Then again, Pacino didn't win for his role in *The Godfather,* so there wasn't much to be said on that front. Further, controversy about the veracity of certain points in *Hurricane* began to surface before the Oscars were handed out, and Washington ultimately lost to Kevin Spacey. The loss would have a chilling impact on Washington's attitude toward Hollywood politics.

Still, Washington continued to make films, even though he admitted to me more than once that he had become jaded, but he surprised many with his performance as a crooked cop in *Training Day.* I hadn't done a piece on him for that film because, quite frankly, Denzel as the bad guy didn't really do it for me. But a dinner and discussion with him, along with Star Jones, Ananda Lewis, and the BET founder, Bob Johnson, after the All-Star NBA game in Washington, D.C., in 2001 led me to believe there was a much more important story that needed to be written about the man.

Shortly after that dinner, I broached the possibility of Denzel as a cover possibility at our weekly editorial meeting in New York. The idea was met with varied degrees of interest, which I understood. From a hard-news standpoint, a cover story would have to address straightforwardly the issue of what race had to do with Washington's failure to receive an Oscar for Best Actor. Race is a delicate subject no matter the industry. But in Hollywood it was swept under the rug with intensity. Few black actors were inclined to discuss in a mainstream publication the limitations placed on them for fear of being blackballed. But I was determined.

I took the idea to Denzel's representatives, and surprisingly, they responded that a story addressing when he'd have his day at the Academy Awards would be welcome. Several interviews around the Christmas holidays in 2001 were scheduled, with me once even making the trip to the San Diego set where he was directing *Antwone Fisher*, the film about a young black man in the navy who is forced to see a psychiatrist to deal with his volatile temper.

It turned out to be no easy feat getting Washington to say on the record what had been so clear at the dinner table ten months before. His disappointment with the industry had been private for years, and getting his views published in *Newsweek* was going to take a certain amount of effort—and patience—on my part. This was one of the reasons I requested numerous interview dates. It would take time for him to find the comfort level needed and to remember the key incidents that had shaped his career and attitude.

A couple of humorous events happened on the way to the story being completed. Our meetings at the L'Ermitage Hotel in Beverly Hills were as colorful as any I can remember. Though we sat in the plush chairs of the eatery just a few feet from the lobby entrance, few recognized the star. He was dressed in his normal attire of a slightly rumpled plaid hunter's jacket, T-shirt, jeans, and a baseball cap pulled low over his forehead. Everyone passed us without a second look. That is, everyone except NBA star John Salley, who politely took a seat between us and talked at length about his new sports show, several times slyly asking Washington to be a guest. Washington, an avid sports fan with courtside seats at the Los Angeles Lakers games, slyly ignored his request. I liked John Salley, with whom I had dealt regularly while covering the Lakers, but I was amazed at how oblivious he was to the fact that an interview was taking place. All I could do was laugh to myself when he finally left, an hour later. The next day, the rapper DMX noticed Washington as we talked and sat down to discuss his admiration for Denzel's work and his own future projects. After he left, we both laughed at the irony of having this happen twice in one week.

Despite the distractions, Washington did begin to open up, divulging tidbits such as John Grisham's unhappiness about his costarring in the film *The Pelican Brief.* It took the actress Julia Roberts to insist that he be cast. "He didn't see the character I played as being black," Washington said of the bestselling author. When I asked Grisham, he denied it. Denzel also discussed his general hesitancy to do love scenes in films and why he'd declined to do a love scene with Roberts in *The Pelican Brief.* Washington said he always kept in mind the feelings of African American women. "Black women are not often seen as objects of desire on film. They have always been my core audience." Early in his career, he'd filmed *The Mighty Quinn,* in which he portrayed a Caribbean police chief in search of a thief. The movie involved a passionate kiss with the white actress Mimi Rogers. The audience response was unpleasant at best, and I remember loudly moaning at the sight of that kiss on the screen. Washington said he learned a valuable lesson at that moment.

We also discussed the movie *Love Field,* in which he was slated to star with Michelle Pfeiffer. The plot revolved around an interracial couple fighting racism during the sixties. Washington was set to be Pfeiffer's lover, until he read the script. "It was nigger this and nigger that. I wasn't going to be but so many niggers in a film," he remembered. Needless to say, the actor backed out of the film, and the part went to the then fledgling actor Dennis Haysbert. Just as Washington had surmised, the role didn't give Haysbert's career a boost, at least not the kind of boost either actor would have desired.

Along with soliciting his own thoughts on his career, I reached out to people Washington had worked with over the years. Celebrities such as Spike Lee, John Singleton, and Lenny Kravitz (one of Washington's closest friends) happily offered up invaluable thoughts on how he got into character, prepared for long shoots, and developed his style onscreen. The boxing promoter Butch Lewis revealed that Washington sometimes has difficulty getting out of character. "Denzel was Malcolm X for three months after the movie stopped filming," Lewis said with a laugh. When I mentioned the comment to Washington, he not only denied but dismissed it with his typical brand of humor. "What? It wasn't like I was going to dinner making speeches like Malcolm, was I?" The actress Cynda Williams, who costarred with Washington in Spike Lee's *Mo' Better Blues,* told me in no uncertain terms that she'd never met Denzel Washington the man. "He was in character for his role as Bleek Gilliam from day one. That was how professional he was from the moment the film began shooting."

But by far the most important people who contributed

to the article were Sidney Poitier and Julia Roberts. Poitier, the epitome of class, sophistication, and style, took great time to discuss how Washington's career mirrored his own in many ways and how he'd always hoped that an actor of Washington's caliber would carry on the mantle of a distinguished body of work, integrity, and respect in film. "Many things have changed in this industry, but many things have remained the same, and it's incredibly disheartening," said Poitier. The incredible burden he'd had as a film actor during the fifties and sixties put Washington's struggle in perspective. I'd never met Poitier before, and even in his seventies, the man was totally mesmerizing in words and presence.

Roberts was more of a riot to talk to. A staunch fan of Washington's, the actress went on and on about how disappointed she was not to have the chance to kiss him in *The Pelican Brief.* She honestly discussed her insistence that he be her costar and how she'd developed a precious relationship with Washington and his wife from that point on. "He should be on his third Oscar by now, and that might not be enough. I mean, did you see *Malcolm* f——ing *X* and *Hurricane* and *Philadelphia*?" she asked rhetorically. But the quote heard around the world was this: "I cannot absorb living in a world where I have an Oscar for Best Actress and Denzel doesn't have one for Best Actor." This declaration of the unfairness of Washington's losses in the Oscar race by the darling of mainstream Hollywood perked up the ears of the people who cast votes at the Academy.

After speaking with Roberts on the phone for about ten minutes, I was speechless when she called me back only five minutes later. She wanted to warn me not to make Washington seem entitled. She didn't want to hurt his chances once again. I thanked her profusely for the tip and noted what a true friend she must be to think so analytically about how the piece could reflect on him.

Writing the story proved to be a stressful two months of dancing carefully around the rarely addressed subject. In retrospect, I can honestly say I didn't know how the story would turn out or how it would be viewed by those in the industry. Calling Hollywood out wasn't Washington's style. I wasn't completely surprised by this. For an African American, it's an unspoken rule that you can't always call a pot a pot. No matter how obvious the pot is. But I brainstormed constantly with friends—some in the business, some not—about how to explain this to *Newsweek* and the mainstream world.

But it was a former costar of Washington's who brought the explanation full circle. The actor, who didn't want his name used then, so I won't use it now, suggested that Washington was much too prideful, too much in charge of his own life to admit that others had any say in it. "To admit that very possibility would be very un-Denzel," the source revealed. This one bit of information was key in giving me the direction I needed to paint a complete picture of the actor. Washington's pride is on full display in each role he's had, as well as each time he's seen in public. But the fact that his pride also seeped into his reaction to inequality had never occurred to me, although it should have, given my twenty-year love affair.

After that realization, my writing moved forward pretty

smoothly. Though the story didn't grace the cover of *Newsweek*, something that was a bit disappointing at the time for me (and for Denzel's publicist, who tore my head off about it), I sometimes think it turned out for the best. The article still received major press and much national attention. *Entertainment Weekly* put the question of race and the Oscars on its cover, with pictures of Washington and his most fierce competitor, Russell Crowe. As is typical with most of my stories, I was worried about Denzel's response. As I mentioned, I had an idea of what I wanted the story to say. However, many times an idea for a story can turn into something totally different when one sits down to write it. I'd soon have my chance to gauge his reaction.

As a major magazine, *Newsweek* is given tickets to the Oscars each year. My editors told me early on that I'd get the tickets to attend. I'd never been so excited, and of course the ritual shopping and beautifying journey began. Let's just say it was a bit more intense than my shopping spree at The Limited when I first interviewed Washington. This time, I needed not one but two dresses, because I would also be attending the "Black Oscars." Though rarely publicized, this is an annual event that pays homage to African American actors. This was to be a special year, since along with Denzel, Halle Berry and Will Smith had been nominated for Academy Awards. Both Washington and Smith attended. Berry opted out for another event.

After the long night, during which any and every African American who had a part in a film won an award, I made my way to the table where Denzel sat with his wife and Samuel L. Jackson and his wife. Naturally, I was nervous. The question raced through my mind: What if he didn't like the story? Would he curse me out right there in front of everybody? But I had to know. Upon seeing me, he reached out and hugged me tightly. He said that it was an amazing article and that he wasn't at all upset he wasn't on the cover. I felt relieved and ready to begin my journey to the Oscars.

The next day was filled with massive confusion and mad running around. I met my editor at his home, where a limo was waiting to take us to the Kodak Theatre in Hollywood. Of course, as fate would have it, our seats were near the back of the auditorium, but I was just happy to be there. When Halle Berry won the award for Best Actress, my stomach dropped. I was worried that her win would lessen Denzel's chances of winning. After all, black actors were still not frequent winners at the Oscars. But then Julia Roberts walked out to present Best Actor, and somehow I knew it was Denzel's night, too. Roberts had won the year before, and it is customary for the previous year's winner to present the current year's award, but it also felt like poetic justice. Denzel just had to win. And he did. You would have thought I won something the way I cheered from my next-to-the-last-row seat.

At the magnificent Governors Ball, the dinner right after the ceremony, I talked to anyone and everyone while I awaited Washington's arrival. The moment he walked through the door and the events that followed are the most compelling reasons I continue to do the work I do. At his table near the front of the beautifully decorated room sat Julia Roberts, Pauletta Washington, and others. I tiptoed up behind him and tapped him on the shoulder for the second night in a row. And for the second night in a row, Washington turned, got out of his seat, and hugged me tightly. But this time he put something in my hand. The Oscar. His Oscar. "You deserve to hold this, because you're part of the reason I won," he said as tears welled up in my eyes. His wife nodded in agreement as my mouth fell open—and stayed open for a good minute. To hear the man I'd fallen in love with at thirteen years old tell me that I had any part of his success was more than I could take.

As I stood there with my knees about to buckle, Washington beckoned Ms. Roberts over to introduce me. She happily told me she'd never had a quote used as much as the one from my story. I was stumped again. Five minutes later, my editor was nudging me to give the Oscar back to Denzel and say good-bye. I finally did, and then got on my cell phone. I woke up my mother in Georgia, aunts in Atlanta, cousins in Virginia. Despite the time difference, no one was safe from my calls that night.

Since that day, I've interviewed Denzel Washington several more times, and he remains one of my favorite subjects. He is the reason I think many journalists do what we do. To write something that changes not only the subject's life but the writer's as well.

Dream Girls

ARETHA, WHITNEY, AND JANET

I still laugh when I think of what one of my aunts said to me when I mentioned I'd be flying to Detroit to interview Aretha Franklin in September 1999: "Finally you're interviewing a real star." Indeed, after several years of interviewing hip-hop's finest, with a few Denzels scattered along the way, meeting the Queen of Soul was destined to be one of the highlights of my entertainment résumé. The Queen had written a book, *Aretha: From These Roots,* about her life as an American icon, and *Newsweek* was interested in hearing more.

Aretha's people arranged for us to meet for lunch at one of her favorite restaurants, near her home on the outskirts of the city. Because of a scheduling glitch, I flew in the morning of the interview, which is never a good thing, given that you have to travel, pick up a rental car, and then find the interview location in a pretty short time.

I'd been to Detroit only once in my life, and that was for a Pistons game. Fortunately, I didn't get too lost and arrived at the eatery about fifteen minutes before the Queen did. And when she did arrive, I was surprised at how taken aback I was by seeing her in the flesh. More than a few other journalists had warned me how difficult Ms. Franklin could be during an interview. The Queen bored easily with questions she'd been asked a million times before and would snap your head off for bringing up a subject she didn't want to talk about. All those thoughts wandered through my head as she moved toward the table I had chosen. She was dressed in a Sunday-go-to-meeting suit, with stockings and heels, and had the mannerisms of any one of my southern-bred aunts. That, along with her dress and the perfume she wore, put me at ease.

I rose to introduce myself while the Queen summoned the waitress to take her order. She was pleasant enough at first. While she made her order—a rather heavy one for midday—she looked at me and said, "I love to eat. You know that." Her blunt declaration helped me segue into what I knew would be a perfect icebreaker. During an interview with me, the superstar Michael Jordan had mentioned that Franklin made the best macaroni and cheese he'd ever tasted. She'd brought him dinner one day after a game in Detroit, and the two remained quite tight. I'd made a mental note of the compliment, tucking it away for some unknown perfect occasion. With that quick mention, the Queen released any reserve she might have had. "What else he say about me, girl?" she demanded.

Loudly laughing, she asked this question a number of times. Much to my chagrin, she was quite serious about wanting to hear other Jordan statements, but I couldn't remember any others worth repeating. Finally, the food came, and we started to talk about her book and her amazing life. It began as the daughter of one of the most famous African American preachers in the country. Her recollections were exact, mostly of sermons her father, the Reverend C. L. Franklin, had preached or of dinners shared with his close friend the Reverend Dr. Martin Luther King, Jr. She also had vivid images of her days on the road with the soul legend Sam Cooke, a man with whom she was truly in love. In the book, she spoke candidly about her crush on the singer and how they almost became lovers one night, but her father interrupted the moment. Her eyes danced as she spoke about the charming crooner, signaling that those may have been the best years of her life.

I also mention the joy in her eyes at that moment because there seemed to be very little of it on the surface of her face that day. Yes, it was clear she'd lived an extraordinary life, but it was also obvious she'd suffered some incredibly painful events, which left her permanently scarred. One of the deepest scars, I'm sure, was the absence of her mother, who'd left the family when Franklin was just three years old. She gives little detail about this loss in her book, but the gospel singer Mavis Staples of the Staple Singers mentioned to me that Franklin kept a brush with her mother's hair still in it on her dresser. This emotional detail explained so much about the soulful feelings in the ripples of Franklin's voice. That one event had shaped the very being of this woman, who in many ways had defined an entire generation.

To warm Franklin up for this potentially explosive subject, I resorted to another of my insider tips, this one from a friend of mine who'd worked in upper management for Nike and shared the fact that Tiger Woods had spent a day teaching the Queen of Soul how to play golf. "Who told you that, girlfriend?" she asked when I brought it up. I didn't know Tiger Woods, so my answer wasn't as fascinating as the Jordan tip, but we'd been chatting it up like old pals for an hour over mashed potatoes, so I asked the serious question anyway.

I referenced the Mavis Staples story, and silence hit the table like a freight train. My intention was certainly not to upset Ms. Franklin, but I felt my question concerned the type of background information her die-hard fans would want to know and understand. Clearly, though, she wasn't ready to share that part of her life yet. From the look on her face, I'm not sure that she ever will be. Fortunately, that tense moment didn't end our interview or earn me a curse-out only the Queen of Soul could deliver. I just moved on.

Since I'm fascinated by old black Hollywood, I kept my composure by grilling her about her days at Atlantic Records and why she'd chosen them over Motown, which was the reigning Detroit record label during her heyday. I was stunned by her admission that she regretted not having someone like the Motown founder, Berry Gordy, guiding her career the way he had so expertly done with Diana Ross. According to Franklin, Gordy had the ability to propel her career to a higher level in all other areas. He could even have put up his fortune to create movie roles for her, as he did with Ms. Ross. Without a powerful mentor, Franklin continued to make hit records, but no other ventures were presented to her. Her personal life was in shambles; she endured a number of destructive relationships with men. There was talk of one of her husbands physically abusing her. Somehow, I gathered enough courage to ask her about it, noting that Ed Bradley had spoke of it on a *60 Minutes* profile of her. Her response was "What does Ed Bradley know?" Exactly. Moving right along.

The rest of the interview went smoothly, with us discussing her well-publicized fear of flying and the trauma of her father's death. Reverend Franklin was shot in an apparent robbery attempt at the Franklins' Detroit home in 1979 and lay in a coma for five years before dying. Franklin's fear of airplanes resulted from flying back and forth between Los Angeles and Detroit weekly to be by his side during that time.

We wrapped up after that. But just as I laughed when I began my journey with Ms. Franklin, I laugh now when I think of the last thing the singer said to me as we waited for her car outside the restaurant. "Why Mavis tell you that stuff about my mother?" I shrugged, hoping not to get a delayed curse-out. But I know Mavis Staples got a funky call that night.

When I think about the great singers of my mother's generation, Aretha definitely comes to mind. Yet when I reflect on the exceptional singers of my generation, I automatically think of Whitney Houston. When Houston blasted on the scene in the mid-eighties, with her beautiful mocha skin, gleaming white smile, and slender frame, the world of music was transformed. She was a breath of fresh air in the

midst of a teen queen moment that had lasted way too long.
I remember the singer from her short-lived modeling days
at *Seventeen,* a time when she rocked a curly, short 'fro and
looked like the sweetest girl next door.

Over the years, Houston became an international sensation, selling millions of records and gracing hundreds of
magazine covers. She also began getting tabloid attention
for her marriage to the music bad boy Bobby Brown. I first
encountered her when she made the movie *The Preacher's
Wife.* It was her third starring role in a film, and she was still
dominating the music charts. Her people arranged for me
to see her in action, first during an international press day
for the movie in New York.

I sat at a table with her while she mesmerized about
thirty Japanese journalists. At this point, she was still seen
as a glamorous diva. Few in the mainstream saw the South
Orange, New Jersey, streak that was firmly embedded in
her personality. That part of her didn't emerge publicly until the famous sit-down with Diane Sawyer years after our
meetings. At our first interview, however, Houston was a
few months pregnant with her second child, a child she
would unfortunately lose.

We sat in her hotel room overlooking Central Park with
various people from her camp coming in and out. Though
the movie was the main focus of our talk, we delved into
other issues, such as the recent death of Tupac Shakur,
whom she considered a good friend. She seemed truly affected by his death and spoke at length about their conversations after his release from prison. This was the Whitney
Houston I think we all loved to see. She was funny, playful,

and full of biblical references that applied to her life as well as her career. We met around Christmastime, so she also talked of her trips with Bobby to Toys "Я" Us and fighting the other parents to buy a Barbie Dream Car for her daughter, Bobbi Christina. It was an image I could only imagine. We ended our talk with a hug and a promise that she would pray for her friend the singer Toni Braxton and me to get husbands in the next year. I think it worked for Toni.

Over the next two years, stories of Whitney's and Bobby's alleged drug use rapidly garnered attention. The rumors were at an all-time high when I sat down to interview her for the second time, in 1998. This was an interview that really rocked my world. It might sound tame now, given what viewers have seen of Whitney on the cable television show *Being Bobby Brown,* but at that time it was something not to be believed. In Ms. Houston's honor, her record label threw an album release party for the press at Mr. Chow in New York. I was seated next to where she would be sitting with the hope that this would warm her up for our one-on-one the next day. Even with all the press there, Houston was a good two hours late. When she did arrive, it was more than clear she wasn't on a natural high. The charming woman with the calm demeanor and a ready scripture quote was no longer present.

As introductions were made, Houston smiled faintly and haphazardly made her way to her chair. We spoke briefly while food was being served, and though she said she remembered our last interview, I found it hard to believe considering the fog she was in. Not deterred, I leaned over midway through our meal and asked what it had been like to work with the producer Wyclef Jean on her new album. Her words at that moment blew me away: "We had a good time. He had his weed and I had my shit and it was all good." I remember just looking at her and thinking, What the hell are you talking about? Don't do this to me, Whitney. Please. The night continued with her drifting in and out of various conversations, making little to no sense.

When it was time to leave, I made my way over to one of the advisers in her camp and, without being specific, quietly told her that it would be in the best interests of all of us if Whitney didn't come to our interview in the same state as she'd been at dinner. I did this for obvious and not so obvious reasons. One, we'd had such a good time and a great interview before that I really wanted to meet *that* woman again. Second, I really needed to ask about the rumors of her drug use, which were quite commonplace in the gossip columns and throughout the music industry. I couldn't very well do that if she weren't, shall we say, herself. The adviser indicated that she completely understood what I meant and would take care of the situation.

The next day I arrived early at the St. Regis Hotel for our three o'clock interview, even though I realized the odds were the singer would be tardy as usual. Surprisingly, she wasn't late, but that was as good as it was going to get. As I sat mulling over my notes, the door opened and Houston flew into the room while shouting to someone behind her, "I don't want to hear that shit," then flung herself in the chair across from mine. She was in exactly the same state she'd been in the night before. All I could think was, "Here we go."

I took it slow, given her state of mind, but an interview is an interview, and I couldn't softball it the entire time. After she talked extensively about some advice the actor Joe Pesci had given her (I have no idea what the advice was because it didn't make much sense), we discussed a variety of appearances she had made that had caused speculation about her health and overall well-being. She explained that the heavy sweating and loss of concentration she had experienced during a recent televised performance were caused by the stress of her late father's illness. A fair answer, and because of that sensible response, I thought we could move nicely into my next question, about the rumors of drug use. I asked if she thought the stress she was under had falsely given the impression she was on drugs. Without skipping a beat, Houston responded, "It's not like me and Bobby are out in the street doing it, and believe me, if it were a big problem, my mother would step in."

My stomach dropped as I leaned over to make sure the tape was still getting her every word. Why couldn't she just have said, "I don't know where the drug rumors come from—they're absurd." That's what celebrities say and do—they deny all and say things are absurd. Still stunned, I recalled an incident the year before when Houston was supposed to appear on Rosie O'Donnell's show. She'd canceled only thirty minutes before the show was to begin and O'Donnell, livid, had publicly implied that Houston had substance abuse issues. Since the singer was being so straightforward with me, I decided to ask about O'Donnell's words, a question I later regretted. Without warning, the true South Orange, New Jersey, girl reared her head. "That fat bitch don't know nothing about me," Houston said, with her head swaying and hands waving. "She needs to shut her big fat mouth."

I let her words just fill the room for a moment, since I had no idea what to say next. We parted ways with a quick hug, but I could instantly tell she'd sobered up enough to know she'd said too much. I had a real dilemma, since so much of the interview was controversial and I really liked her as a person and an artist. But my problems were only just beginning. I decided to walk from the hotel to the *Newsweek* offices to clear my head. When I made it back to work, my editor was waiting just outside my office. Houston's publicist had already called and explained that the singer had said many things she didn't mean and that we couldn't print them. To make matters worse, she had another appearance scheduled on O'Donnell's show the very next week.

As you might expect, *Newsweek* doesn't respond well to being told what to print, and in truth, until that point it was my decision what to use in the story. But Houston's publicist had taken that option away by giving my editors the more salacious details of our interview. After a few meetings with the top editors at the magazine, we decided not to use Houston's quote "fat bitch" referencing O'Donnell since many of Houston's fans did not know that side of her and it was such a demeaning statement. Furthermore, Houston was clearly not in her right mind. Her comments about her use of drugs and what she thought about the rumors stayed in the piece, and I was comfortable with that. I'd given her people the chance to postpone the interview until she was in better shape. Nonetheless, Houston's people were none too pleased with the printed product, and of course, I felt bad.

Needless to say, I've not interviewed Ms. Houston since that story ran (I have talked to Mr. Brown a number of times since, and he's highly entertaining), but I did get an eerie sensation of déjà vu while watching her and Bobby act like fools during the interview with Diane Sawyer. And, having watched a few episodes of *Being Bobby Brown,* I see clearly that the woman I met ten years ago is now completely gone. Still, there may be hope for Whitney Houston. Ironically, late last year Houston found the strength to face down one of her demons by filing for divorce from longtime husband, Bobby Brown, and reuniting with former mentor Clive Davis. With a clear future and the absence of dead weight, we might actually get to celebrate that stunning woman with the amazing voice once again. After all, there's nothing we love better than a triumphant comeback story. No doubt the world will embrace her with open arms.

It might seem a bit disrespectful to include Janet Jackson alongside the likes of Aretha Franklin and Whitney Houston, but while Ms. Jackson may not have the vocal strength of those women, she's every bit as much a diva. For most of my life, the name Jackson was larger than life in the entertainment world. But it was adorable Janet to whom I most related. From her role on *Good Times* to her hypnotic videos and flawless hair weaves, Jackson mesmerized not only me but the world. So when the album *The Velvet Rope* was about to be released in 1997, I jumped at the chance to do a review and talk with the singer.

Unfortunately, it wasn't that easy a task. One of Jackson's publicists wanted a *Newsweek* cover based on her many body piercings while another wanted some other special provision that the magazine couldn't provide. Just when I thought the story was dead in the water, Jackson fired those publicists, and an interview was set up only a week before the album's release. I arrived on time. Her then husband, Rene Elizondo, opened the door of her trailer and welcomed me into a small room with colorful roses placed all around. Tall, with a deep olive complexion and dark, curly hair, Rene was exceedingly polite. He apologized for all the drama I'd been put through in obtaining the interview and then left to get his wife from a video shoot.

Ms. Jackson walked into the room with that deeply dimpled smile that had made her so cute as a girl on television, dressed down in jeans and a T-shirt. Her hair was braided in two thick ponytails, and she was her preferred slim size four. Just as her husband had, she apologized profusely for what I'd experienced over the last few weeks and began to explain why she'd fired her publicists. I assured her this happened all the time, and we began our intense four-hour interview.

Surprisingly, she was more than happy to rehash her childhood for me. Many celebrities who have been around for a while and have stories as famous as that of the Jackson family hate to backtrack. But Janet spoke at length about going to dance classes and being taunted for her huge rear end, by a teacher no less. She remembered not being able to spend the night with friends because of her family's fame and how she'd stop calling her father Dad. I wanted to ask her the reason why she'd stopped calling her father Dad at such a young age, but I could tell that she wasn't going to say anything more.

I mentioned the rumors that continued to swirl that as a teenager she'd had a child with her first husband, James DeBarge. She laughed a girlish giggle and said she'd heard that one, too. She never denied it—just said she'd heard the rumor. We then dealt with her relationship with her older brother Michael, and she admitted not having spoken to him in a year or more. I was stunned, and even more amazed by her reason. She said he'd been out of the country a lot over the last few years. They didn't have phones where he was? I asked. She never really gave me an answer. She spoke lovingly of her mother, Katherine, whom she said kept the family connected, and how she talked with her nearly every day. Her face glowed as she discussed recently becoming close with her big sister LaToya again after the family ended a rift with the older daughter.

The singer also talked about suffering from depression for a few years and the way it had affected her weight and everything else. Her explanation of how she'd work out for four or five hours a day, sometimes for months, then not work out at all for months because she was burned out made perfect sense to me. I asked how she'd overcome her depression, since it's such a difficult and misunderstood illness. Oddly enough, she told me of a guru she'd met who'd taken her to the desert to meditate and also suggested she get regular coffee enemas to recharge her system. Yes, coffee enemas. How she'd regret telling me that piece of information.

I had little time to think of what it meant or how it would be received when put into print. This was my typical problem—celebrities becoming way too comfortable in an interview and then thinking I would censor their words for their best interests. We continued to talk about Jackson's album and what she'd done to get it made in the middle of feeling down. I really liked her and had a ball with the interview. She was exactly as I'd expected her to be—soft-spoken, a little shy, and incredibly driven in her career.

I sent the interview tapes out to be transcribed since I had hours of tape and the story was due that week. The editors decided to run the interview as a question-and-answer piece since Jackson had spoken candidly about so many different things. The Friday night before the magazine hit the stands, I pored over the contents of the Q & A, hoping to catch anything that seemed a little too much. The lawyers had removed Jackson's references to her father, and space had required we cut out many other things as well. All in all, I liked the finished product, but I was not at all prepared for what was to come.

The comedian Jay Leno used the coffee enema quote to make merciless fun of the singer on his late-night show. Jackson was not amused. Oprah Winfrey's producers called to request several copies of the article because the singer would be a guest on her show that week. I was not looking forward to hearing Jackson's thoughts about our chat or its end result. Indeed, her *Oprah* appearance focused a great deal on the article, with her saying she didn't mean things that way or not exactly that way. I felt for her, but again, what could I do? On the flip side, my mother and aunts called the entire day, overjoyed that they'd seen Oprah hold up an article with my name on it. I could die now.

The good thing is that I've seen Janet Jackson a number of times since the story ran, and it's been all good. There was no way for her—or me—to know how the article would be perceived. I think with time she understood. I often wonder if the fact that she was a Jackson played into the way her comments were made fun of. But on the real, a coffee enema is a pretty damn funny story. Sorry, Janet. Yet maybe it's Janet who's getting the last laugh, since those coffee enemas might just be one of the reasons she looks absolutely fabulous as she fashionably glides into her forties.

Let Me Ride

The words came down like a hammer. Not guilty. With just the sound of those two words voiced in a Los Angeles courtroom, Calvin Broadus, a.k.a. Snoop Dogg, became a free man. The look on his face at the moment was one of true happiness, something only those who've been behind bars can understand. I breathed a sigh of relief as well, because I'd covered Snoop for several years before his arrest and liked him a great deal. I had no idea whether he was guilty of the murder he was accused of. He was a reputed gang member, a gangsta rapper, and God only knows what else. But I had this thing about Snoop and the people who made up his world at Death Row Records.

It's funny because nothing—and I mean absolutely nothing—I experienced growing up in Augusta, Georgia, could have prepared me for my days with and around Death Row. Death Row Records is a label founded in 1991 by the rapper-producer Andre "Dr. Dre" Young and the infamous Marion "Suge" Knight. That a rap record label, founded by two men who grew up not only thousands of miles but worlds apart from me, would ultimately have such an impact on my career and life is something no one could have convinced me of just the year before. Then again, the year before I was blowing up plastic dinosaurs for Steven Spielberg at Creative Artists Agency, something else no one could have convinced me I'd be doing. But moving on.

My dealings with the three most visible men of the seminal record company were as varied as the personalities of the men themselves. I met each at very different times in my career and theirs, before and during my time at *Newsweek*. Each relationship has developed full circle in one way or another as the years have passed on.

Given his larger than life personality, it's hard to admit that I don't remember exactly how or where I met Calvin Broadus for the first time. It's particularly bizarre since, out of all the celebrities I've dealt with in the last twelve years, Snoop and the posse that surrounds him win the "over the top" award hands down, year after year.

No one should wonder why few can outdo a man whose coal black hair is longer and prettier than that of the most glamorous woman on the cover of any fashion magazine. And few have the power to erase the memories of a man whose very scent could rob you of your breath the minute he enters the room. For those who don't know, Snoop Dogg loves weed, a fact he's established over the years in videos, on album covers, and by usually having enough of the stuff on him to supply an entire small country. That's why most

of my visits with the Long Beach, California, native ended
up with the ritual airing out of my clothes on the balcony
of my apartment for no fewer than three days.

Yet that was Snoop's charm and an added bonus for me
as a writer, because it gave a distinctly authentic undertone
to each story I wrote about him. With his comical, laid-
back approach to anything and everything in life, Snoop
was often a bright spot during some often difficult times
writing about Death Row and hip-hop in general.

The first time I got a true feel for Snoop was during the
period surrounding the murder trial, which was for sure one
of the lowest points in his life. The trial, which began in late
1995, put him and his bodyguard, McKinley Lee, in the
forefront of the media; they were charged with the first-
degree murder of a Long Beach gang member named Phil-
lip Woldemariam in 1993. For better or worse, Snoop never
shied away from admitting his longtime affiliation with the
Crips gang, an entity I got to know pretty well through my
stories on him and others in the world of West Coast rap.
As if from a movie script, his past life had come back to
haunt him with devastating results.

The trial lasted a few weeks, each day an exhausting ex-
ercise in contradictions, incompetency (bullets and other
crucial evidence were lost by police officers), and baffled
jurors, who had little idea what gang life was about. I still
remember being in the courtroom the day the verdict was
handed down for Snoop and Lee and watching as Snoop
humbly gave thanks up above for his freedom.

Not surprisingly, it was chaos in and around the courtroom shortly after, with everyone from the record label as
well as family and friends trying to get a moment with the

Doggfather. In between hugs and whispers of congratulations, George Pryce, then the charismatic public relations person for Death Row, who had a penchant for boldly colored suits and oversize rock-star glasses, caught my attention. He pulled me aside, saying, "Snoop's having a little party at Monty's with the whole gang. Don't spread it, but come through if you can around nine P.M."

Papa G, as George was affectionately known within the Death Row camp, had been a wealth of information for me while I was covering the controversial record label. He was completely dependable for tidbits and lively descriptions of who did what and where all around the industry. He also advised me on the best times to deal with his popular and often troubled artists.

Over the years, many of my journalism and nonjournalism friends have questioned my alliance to a label that was known for violence and degrading portrayals of women. While I never endorsed the message of the music, I had a job to do, and it required a completely objective mind-set. As a matter of fact, I've experienced a number of unpleasant situations with famous artists, but none of them were ever with the likes of Dr. Dre, Snoop, or Tupac. Suge Knight was also perfectly pleasant to me every time I encountered him. For example, he called me one day to let me know that *Newsweek* fact checkers were calling to verify the information in my story on him. He wasn't familiar with the editorial process of major magazines (they usually have researchers to double-check information) and considered this a way of *Newsweek* trying to "take a sistah down." I thanked him profusely for the heads-up.

The party spot Monty's was an obvious choice for the

celebration. The swanky eatery in the Westwood section of Los Angeles, near UCLA, had been the "it" spot for Suge Knight and his ever-expanding crew for years. Monty's was dimly lit, with several secluded rooms and employees who seemed to understand their customers' need for complete privacy. Knight and posse would often post up there at all times of night, feasting on the eatery's extensive selection of grilled steaks and exotic seafood.

As soon as Pryce told me of the party, I mentally began to prepare myself. I'd been to my share of "Tha Row" events over the years, and those experiences had forced me to create a short list of necessities. I made most of these trips alone, since most of my girlfriends—and guy friends—ever so politely declined when I extended them invitations. This made my list even more important. Number one: Wear sneakers or flat shoes, because a woman cannot run from a shooting, fight, or stomp-down in her Manolos, Jimmy Choos, Charles Davids, or even Nine Wests. Two: Survey the room upon entering to make sure you know the surest and fastest way out in case one or all of the previously mentioned events occurs. Three: Sit close (but not too close) to one of Knight's posse members to gain the early scoop on when to get ghost.

You might ask why it took me so long to figure this out. Or better yet, why go through the trouble at all? Stupidity, that's why. It was plain stupidity, mixed with a sincere desire to write with clarity and understanding about a culture that was dominating the mainstream before the mainstream ever knew what hit it.

It's hard to shake a childhood in the Deep South, where

gang wasn't a term ever used. I grew up attending school dances, frequenting Jack and Jill parties at which I can hardly remember the raising of voices, much less full-on fights. So imagine my surprise when I attended one of my first Death Row parties and didn't realize someone had been stomped to death on the dance floor until I heard the sirens on my way to my car. I jammed on that dance floor the entire night without so much as a clue.

So on this night, with all my must-haves in check, I arrived at Monty's around 10:00 P.M. and happily found that the then MTV correspondent Alison Stewart and I were the only media in attendance. The guys at Death Row had always been pretty loyal to me when it came to handing out juicy stories. Even at that point in 1996, various major media outlets were angling for a chance to look inside the world of the embattled label. Because of *Newsweek*'s constant coverage, during the good and the bad times, and my established relationships with the guys on the label, I often got first dibs on stories without asking. This access helped a lot in my career at the magazine and as a developing hip-hop reporter and commentator.

Scanning the room for exits, I recognized the usual suspects at Death Row functions—Suge Knight, along with his pals Bountry, Neckbone, Bustop, and Heiron, and the artists Tupac, Hammer, Kurupt, and Daz. Snoop and his adorable son Corde (a.k.a. Spanky) were greeting each guest at the door with smiles and hugs. Spanky, up way past his two-year-old's bedtime, was even doing a celebratory dance on the front tables. As for Dr. Dre, at that point, the cofounder was slowly easing his way out of the company, so his appearances at events connected to Death Row were few and far between.

As the music of familiar artists played in the background and a tasty dinner of lobster, steak, and crab legs was being served at tables, other guests began to arrive, and trust me when I say they were anything but typical. Middle-aged and older white men and women began filling up the intimately cornered-off dining space in droves. Looking out of place and slightly frightened at first, the group eventually began mingling happily with the likes of Tupac, Hammer, and Snoop.

Soon cameras were being pulled out and autographs distributed like candy on Halloween. An eerie vibe of "We Are Family" filled the room. When an obviously drunk fifty-something white male took the microphone at the front of the room and began to deliver an ill-advised and unfortunate freestyle rap, it suddenly hit me that I'd seen these faces before. The more the man rapped, the more I was able to connect the dots. These were the jurors from Snoop's trial.

To say that seeing the men and women who'd only hours before given Snoop his freedom at a party for him was a surprise would be an incredible understatement. But if I'd learned one thing over the years of covering the record label, it was always to expect the unexpected.

For the rest of the night, I watched in varying degrees of disbelief from my table, with my dinner companions Bustop and Bountry, who proceeded to eat the crab legs off my plate. At Suge's behest, Hammer began performing his rusty, slightly buffoonish dance moves to amuse the partygoers. And, boy, were they amused. If that wasn't enough,

Snoop was moving around the room in a sort of slow-motion trance, no doubt in a chronic haze.

But by far the most interesting guest that night was Tupac. He'd been a regular at Snoop's trial, even though he'd just been released from prison himself. While most were celebrating, Tupac stood near the DJ table staring blankly into space as madness swirled around him. 'Pac's face was rarely devoid of emotion, but on this particular occasion he seemed truly perplexed at what had to look like a bad night at the Apollo. I often wonder what the then twenty-four-year-old rapper was thinking that night. In less than six months he would be dead. I never got the chance to ask.

I often think about that party and the sad reality of what's happened since. Tupac was killed famously in Vegas. Bountry, Heiron, and Bustop, too, have all since been killed, no doubt results of gang warfare. For all the times I dealt with Bountry, Neckbone, and the crew, I never knew their real names, so I found out about their deaths sometimes years later. Yet whenever I get a little sentimental about that night, I just pull out the cover of *Death Row Greatest Hits*. Inside the flap is a picture of myself and Bustop, no doubt discussing the involuntary dispensing of my crab legs, and it gives me a quick laugh.

But back to a lighter note on Snoop. One of my other favorite Snoop moments was his wedding in 1997 to his high school sweetheart, Shante. Snoop is a man of simple taste when it comes to certain things, and his low-key back-yard wedding was a jarring example of that fact. Despite minimal decorations, a cash bar, and a metal detector, the wedding of the Doggfather and his bride was quite a touching affair. His then three-year-old son, Corde, pimp-walked his way down the aisle as the ring bearer, and Snoop's long locks were styled in the most gorgeous Shirley Temple curls I'd ever seen. Proving my point about the beauty of Snoop's tresses, his bride's coiffed hairstyle paled in comparison, and she seemed to be painfully aware of it.

The gift room was filled to overflowing with packages. It didn't hurt that one of the couple's wedding stores of choice was Target. Drinking out of foam cups offered a certain down-home comfort at the reception.

Stomachaching moments with Snoop were endless, and just when I thought there couldn't be any more, he'd give me another dose. In August 1996, just weeks before Tupac's death, Snoop was putting the finishing touches on his second album after a year of constant turmoil. Papa G called to tell me that Snoop might be heading to Vegas for the Mike Tyson fight, so I needed to interview him soon about his new music. He was recording in the San Fernando Valley.

It's hotter than hell in the San Fernando Valley in late August, but that was where Snoop was, so I made the long, dreary trek to the Woodland Hills studio. He'd been laying down the final tracks for his album for a few months with a bevy of new and old producers. The lanky star was peering out the window when I pulled up around two o'clock that afternoon. He motioned that it was okay for me to park right there in front of the studio. It's worth noting that the studio was on the famous Ventura Boulevard, one of the best-known, if not most used streets in California, but still I didn't give a second thought to parking there since Snoop had said it was okay. Back to that in a minute.

I was anxious to get the interview under way since Snoop was always a hoot to talk to, and I knew that his signature lazy southern-style drawl laced over music would be bound to have one or two hits. Inside the studio's "chill room," complete with the required black leather couch, were the lovable DJ Pooh (best known for writing and appearing in the film *Friday*) and a face that I'd never seen before, a character named Lil' Black Malik. I was pretty sure I'd met most of the people who made up Death Row, but Lil' Black Malik was new to me. It seemed the studio already had a producer named Malik, so Snoop decided a distinction had to be made. "We kept getting those motha———kers mixed up," he said. "You call one, and the other one would answer. That was tiring shit."

Lil' Black Malik was indeed dark in hue and petite in size, hence his name, but he had a personality big enough to fill two notebooks. Too bad I had no idea what he did or why he was there. With Snoop offering colorful one-liners about the past year of his life, Lil' Black Malik would contribute statements that further illustrated his point. If Snoop lost his train of thought while explaining a track on the album, Lil' Black Malik would pipe in with the needed details with a knowing expertise. His fluid commentary gave Snoop a chance to take his numerous breaks. All afternoon, the two played word-for-word tag team, and it worked quite well for me and the story.

Three hours and a couple of head rushes later, I was done. I hugged Snoop and thanked Lil' Black Malik, whom I never saw again—nor was he ever mentioned again—and packed my recorder to head back to the office. I reached the street, and not a car was in sight, including mine. The absence of my car meant it had been towed (because no one would have stolen a junky Honda Civic). The sign a few feet ahead plainly gave notice that cars parked after 4:00 P.M. would be towed. I must have been high myself listening to Snoop. And with just twenty bucks in my Coach bag, getting my car *untowed* was going to require some assistance.

The assumption here might be that, as a journalist at a major magazine, I'd just call a cab or car service to drive me to the tow yard. Let me explain why this was easier said than done. First, let's dispel the myth that print reporters make a wad of dough. We do *not*. And when you couple that fact with my crazy shoe habit, an embarrassing jeans fetish (I own over a hundred pairs), and a weekly nonnegotiable black woman hair appointment, it becomes a bit clearer why extra cash—$250—wasn't just lying at the bottom of this reporter's purse.

So after having a deserved mini-meltdown, I collected myself and sheepishly walked back to the studio. After a few hard knocks, Pooh opened the door with a big I-feel-no-pain look on his face. It seemed in my short absence there had been a massive chronic break, so I had to hold on to the wall to keep my balance as I walked through the fog-like smoke to the chill room. Lil' Black Malik and Snoop hadn't moved from the black leather couch, though now their eyes were barely open and the smiles were even wider across their faces.

While breathing out of my nose, I explained my dilemma to them, and before I knew it, a wide-brimmed black hat was being passed around like a Sunday morning church collection plate. Snoop put in the biggest chunk of cash (guilt, no doubt, though he stressed it was his extra weed money) and proceeded to drive me in his lowrider to the tow yard, five miles away. I'll never forget walking up to the window of the tow yard office and watching the elderly owner stare at the heavy-lidded rapper behind me. Snoop was waving at him or throwing up gang signs or both, I could never really tell. All I know is that the poor guy was still staring as Snoop and I drove off in different directions.

Later that week, *Newsweek* sent a check written to Snoop Doggy Dogg to reimburse Snoop for getting my car. Unfortunately, it never occurred to our accounting department that Charles Schulz and, more important, Snoop's mother, would have thought it in poor taste actually to name a human being after a cartoon animal. We corrected it, though, with a check written out to Calvin Broadus just a few days later.

With our numerous sit-downs, Snoop and I always seemed to have a certain understanding. But Snoop was still Snoop, and one could never be completely sure how he'd show up for an event, meaning high or not high, curls or no curls. The good thing, though, was that you knew he'd show up. But because of his alternating styles of arrival, I've always made it a point to attend the photo sessions he's done with the magazine. Normally I don't do this, but with certain subjects you can't leave anything to chance.

One infamous photo shoot with the Doggfather happened at his hotel in New York City. To my chagrin, and even though it was just ten in the morning, Snoop was floating and happily doing a Crip dance for the very satisfied photographer. I could only stand on the side and wonder how to stop the madness. Fortunately, Snoop saw the expression on my face and asked earnestly, "What's wrong, Ma?"

Now things can get tricky in situations like this. You want artists to be true to themselves and their background, but at the same time, *Newsweek* is a major news publication with stories that reach both national and international audiences. Snoop's ode to his gang ties sent chills down my spine as I imagined the hundreds of letters I'd get from angry black folks asking why I'd let the rapper carry on in such a stereotypical way. I'll never forget receiving similar angry letters when we photographed the rapper Ice Cube holding up the sign for Westside with his fingers. It was not a gang sign at all, but a young black male holding any sign with his fingers was automatically cause for concern. And now here was Snoop being visually captured doing a full-on gangbanger dance.

With as stern a voice as I could muster, I calmly informed Snoop that this photo shoot was not for a hip-hop magazine, where there probably wouldn't be a backlash. Also, I told him that in all likelihood his fellow Crip members would not see his shout-out, however thoughtful. He seemed to get the message, that is, until he began blowing marijuana rings into the camera, requiring another sideline meeting. Fortunately, he complied the second time as well, and the rest of the shoot went off without a hitch.

Over the years I've been surrounded by a slew of Snoop's friends during and after interviews. While he was filming his short-lived MTV show, I met with Snoop on the set in Santa Monica. This was soon after his much publicized declaration that he'd stopped smoking weed, something many mainstream publications actually covered with straight faces. I, however, never took this seriously, and I doubt anyone who knew Snoop did. A man who's smoked weed for most of his life does not just stop using it one day unless he's on his way to Betty Ford. Snoop was not going to Betty Ford.

Snoop's trailer on the MTV lot was a haven of luxury, with a state-of-the-art stereo, fully equipped kitchen, and a huge flat-screen TV with full access to all of the rapper's favorite Los Angeles Lakers games. Upon entering his mobile abode, I saw good old DJ Pooh again and two new faces—Bishop Don Juan, the onetime pimp, and the former NBA player Isaiah Rider. For NBA heads in the know, it's common knowledge that wherever Rider goes, weed (and possibly illegal cell phones) follow, and this day was no exception. The trailer, though luxe, was pretty small, which forced me to walk outside every ten minutes to ensure I could drive home without being pulled over. Keeping the door open would have lulled half of Santa Monica to sleep.

Without shame or concern that a news reporter was in his midst, Snoop passed around a blunt so big it looked like the root of a large tree. When I asked where the crazy idea that he had stopped smoking came from, he looked at me with his patented smile and said, "You know," while the trailer rocked with laughter.

My brief introduction to Bishop Don Juan that night led to a longer phone conversation about his relationship with Snoop. The Chicago native was indeed a former pimp who still had a penchant for outrageously loud clothes and diamonds galore. Nonetheless he could be downright fatherly in describing how he'd asked Snoop to stop showing up to business meetings high: "I told him you can't handle no business like that." Our friendly exchange went on for more than an hour while he discussed his other clients P. Diddy and Mike Tyson. He also made provisions for me to receive his book, *From the Pimpstick to the Pulpit*. Years later, I still haven't been able to read it, though I keep it around just in case I need some literary inspiration.

I'd apparently made an impression on the Bishop, because two weeks after my story on Snoop ran in *Newsweek*, he called my office out of the blue. This time he was in need of my services. It seemed that he had not received his consultant check for his work on the film *Starsky & Hutch*, where he'd advised Snoop on how to portray Huggy Bear. For some reason, Snoop had suggested I might be able to help the Bishop retrieve his money, which was more evidence to me that Snoop needed to put the blunts down. I quickly suggested to the Bishop that he call his lawyer or agent because there was little I could do.

Despite my lack of assistance, the Bishop cordially invited me to the Player's Ball in Chicago, the annual party for pimps. His description of the event made it sound like the social event of the year. I'm not sure if I should have been insulted or not by the invite, since the ball primarily attracts pimps and hos, but I graciously turned him down. Death Row parties were one thing, but pimp conventions were definitely not in my job description. I never found out if the Bishop got his money, but I can't imagine a former pimp being pimped.

• • •

For all the outrageous glory that is Snoop, Andre Young, a.k.a. Dr. Dre, was a completely different story. While tales of his infamous assaults on people, such as television show host Dee Barnes, made him appear to be one of the more unsavory characters in the music business during the early nineties, I fortunately never met that man. Calm, polite, and pleasant to a fault, my Dr. Dre interviews are among my favorites from my years as a journalist. Part of the reason is, of course, the music that he's created over the last twenty years. His hypnotic West Coast beats have defined an entire generation and influenced hip-hop culture in countless ways. But there was another factor that made Dre a fascinating character profile no matter how many times you talked to him. He has an amazing ability to get up and out of bad situations without ever looking back.

I initially met Dre while I was a reporter at the *Los Angeles Times* and he was still a part of the seminal rap group N.W.A. I was working the courthouse beat at the paper, and that involved going through the hundreds of complaints and lawsuits filed in the Orange County courthouse looking for anything newsworthy. I was familiar with N.W.A., but their explicit lyrics back then kept them off my regular listening list, and I certainly had no idea at the time that Dr. Dre's real name was Andre Young. A lawyer friend of mine brought his case to my attention. It involved a young mother accusing Dre of giving her less than one hundred dollars (and one bag of diapers) for the twelve-month-old who had proven to be his.

In my journalistic capacity, I reached out to the young producer for a comment about his lack of parental duty. We talked via telephone, and let's just say his response was unprintable. Not wanting to muddy his character completely, I left his colorful commentary out of my story but mentioned his contribution to a popular song that criticized gang violence. It wasn't much, but it softened an ugly tale about a famous guy with a lot of money not taking care of his own.

The newspaper ran with it, because in Orange County stories on black celebrities were few and far between. I gave our photo department very clear instructions on who Dre was on the N.W.A. album cover from which they cropped his image, yet they still managed to run a picture of Ice Cube instead. Not only was that grounds for a lawsuit but it was grounds for a good ass-whopping. Notably mine.

As any reporter will tell you, we have nothing to do with the photos used to complement stories. Once I pointed out Dre to the photo editor, I was done. Whatever went wrong after that didn't involve me. Despite it all, I knew that with my solo name on the story, I'd be the obvious target of anger from a group of guys who had scared America to death with their radically rebellious music. To prevent the possibility of bodily harm to me, I reached out to Dr. Dre and Ice Cube as soon as I realized the mistake. Dre found the entire thing hilarious, and Cube couldn't have cared less about what a newspaper in Orange County said or didn't say.

As scary as that was, I ended up developing an honest, forthcoming relationship with Dre, which made the articles I wrote on him some of my most insightful work. It's a relationship that's lasted through the formation of Death Row Records and the release of all his subsequent successful work. It has also witnessed some pretty perilous times in the life of the rapper-producer, especially his decision to get involved with Suge Knight.

Dre's decision to join forces with Knight proved to be the equivalent of shaking hands with the devil, and Dre figured that out much sooner than most people realized. Rumors of all types of scandalous actions were being passed around the industry from the moment he and Knight set up shop. While the hits kept coming, Dre was less and less visible on the company front. Having experienced enough chaos in his early career, he seemed to know where the company was heading and wanted no part of it. "You take a seventeen-year-old from the ghetto and give him six or seven figures, and you're going to get some out-of-control shit happening. But I've definitely matured in the last five years," he told me for a story called "How Dr. Dre Plans to Become the Quincy Jones of Rap."

One of the final straws for Dre's departure was the arrival of Tupac Shakur in late 1995. Knight and the label had sprung for the rapper's release from prison. With his gregarious personality, in-your-face style, and massive talent, Tupac quickly forced his way to the center of attention at the company. No small feat, given Death Row's colorful roster. But as tensions between Dre and Knight festered, Tupac happily poured gasoline on the fire.

The rapper started criticizing Dre at every turn, even publicly scolding him for not attending Snoop's murder trial and for his lack of participation in other Death Row events. This was a sharp change for the two men who had previously enjoyed a very civil relationship. Disarmingly bright, Tupac was a masterful chameleon and routinely became the same as whoever he was around, which meant also taking on other people's demons and battles. In this case, they were Suge Knight's.

One of my most fond memories of Dre was in Calabasas in early 1996. He'd just had his California home redecorated with deep purple hues and jazz motifs. We spent the day walking around talking about old times, his last time seeing Eazy-E before his death, and his complicated relationships with the other remaining members of N.W.A.

As the day wore on, we made our way to his basement studio, and he put on a track for me that he'd just completed. It was a mesmerizing tune that immediately got your head moving and feet tapping. Massive chart topper was written all over it. It was the music for "California Love," with no Tupac vocals at all. Dre had planned to put the song, sans Tupac, on his new solo album, due out later that year. Somewhere along the way, Knight had heard the track and decided Tupac would be better suited for the music. Knight was the head of the label, and what he wanted he got, and what he wanted was to get under Dre's skin. Dre was not happy about it, yet both rappers ended up on the track, and it indeed became a hip-hop classic. Still, it ended a chapter in Dre's musical career. He gave up everything connected to Death Row Records shortly after and, in true Dre style, never looked back.

• • •

Suggesting Suge Knight as a feature subject to my editor during my first few weeks at *Newsweek* was a very funny moment for me. No one there had ever heard of the towering figure of a man. I'd only met him briefly during a label reception, but I knew he'd be a great story. I interviewed him for the first time in Orlando, Florida, while at the now defunct Jack the Rapper music industry convention. During that weekend, I witnessed the many sides of Suge Knight. I watched him start or engage in a number of fights, mesmerize a group of record executives, and charm whoever he desired at the moment. Our interview went well, but then came the chore of getting him to pose for pictures. These were the days before Knight became a household name and before he began to enjoy the national spotlight he'd come to cherish at all costs. It would eventually be his downfall.

After days of haggling, Knight posed wearing a bright red plaid shirt leaning back on a 1964 lowrider on Crenshaw Boulevard in South Central. Just like that, a legend was born. Many of his cohorts to this day blame *Newsweek* for giving him the massive publicity that he eventually couldn't get enough of. I take partial responsibility, but given the nature of the business, the impact of the hits his company was putting out, and his larger-than-life personality, Suge Knight was going to be noticed.

I saw Knight numerous times over the last few years of the company's existence. He invited me to his annual Mother's Day events, his Christmas parties, and even the opening of his popular Club 662 in Las Vegas (662 spells MOB on the phone pad in case you're wondering). For all the stories that are told about Suge Knight, the most interesting by far for me was meeting his parents. Two delightful southern-born people who seemed to be no relation to the man considered a menace to the entertainment industry. We met at a Compton Denny's in South Central Los Angeles one morning for breakfast complete with eggs and bacon. I was working on a story about their son (he was in prison at the time), and his parents agreed to discuss the "truth" about him. His mother told stories of Christmas toys, school plays, and the fact that she'd named him Sugar—Suge for short—when he was born because he was such a sweet baby. I remember leaving the eatery marveling at how strong a mother's love could be.

Black Cat

Michael Jordan

There are people who charm. There are people who mesmerize. And trust me when I say that the NBA legend Michael Jordan is very adept at doing both. I'd never been much of a fan of Air Jordan before I met him in 1995, partially because of my Detroit Pistons alliance and partially because the only other NBA team that was sanctioned in my family was the Los Angeles Lakers, despite the fact that few of my family had ever set foot in California.

There were other reasons for my not being a fan of Jordan, most notably the air of arrogance I always sensed in him after a win or the controversy that surrounded the exorbitant price of his Nike sneakers, which resulted in several inner-city kids committing murder for a pair. Last, there was his glaring failure to support the candidate running against the known racist Jesse Helms for the U.S. Senate in Jordan's home state of North Carolina in the early nineties. But don't think I didn't have my priorities straight.

The true nail in the coffin came in 1991, when Jordan's

storied Chicago Bulls eliminated the Pistons from the NBA semifinals. I was so annoyed I vowed to never watch His Airness pick up a ball again. So, of course, I didn't bother batting an eye in 1993 when Jordan retired prematurely (after his father's murder), though many of my girlfriends were so heartbroken you'd have thought they'd been ditched at the altar on the day of their wedding.

I paid equally little attention when he returned to the court in 1995. At that point, most of my favorite players were out of the game, so the NBA didn't much matter to me. But a good girlfriend of mine decided I needed to make the most of my sports-reporting résumé (with only Mike Tyson on it) by flying to Chicago to see the Bulls play in person. This friend also offered an introduction with the hope of my getting an interview with the player about his return. I agreed, mainly because I'd never been to Chicago and wanted to see the Water Tower, because of course, that was where Oprah lived.

We were set up for a Saturday afternoon game, and my girlfriend, who knew quite a few NBA players, had played it slick by requesting tickets from both Jordan and a player on the opposing team. Lo and behold, Jordan's tickets were better (just behind courtside), so she ended up scalping the other ones for a wad of cash just before tip-off.

Seeing Jordan play in the flesh while he was still in his prime is a memory that will stay at the top of my best-ever list. Television could do little justice to the art Jordan created on the hardwood for all those years. I was almost sorry that I'd spent the better part of his career not being a fan. After the game ended, my girlfriend and I made our way toward the locker room. Since I'd never been in any locker room, much less that of a major sports team, I hung back as she positioned herself to get Jordan's attention as soon as he came into view.

Looking very dapper in a brown tailor-made suit, with his flawless ebony skin and shining bald head, Black Cat, a name many inside his circle call him, glided down the hallway with a throng of cameras, tape recorders, and just plain mass hysteria nipping at his heels. I was overwhelmed at the scene and even more overwhelmed at Jordan's calm demeanor. He stopped to give my friend a hug, and the two chatted for a few moments before she introduced me. The arrogance I'd sensed so many times oozing from my television set quickly faded as this towering (very, very fine) man firmly took my hand and told me how nice it was to meet me.

I know it sounds lame, but I heard and saw genuine sincerity in his voice and posture when he spoke those words, and that for sure was not the norm for someone of his stature. I had interviewed enough celebs by that point to know the difference. But that was how he got you. He became and stayed that man all those years. Before meeting Jordan that day, I'd read how he kept bad press away with the way he handled people. He'd make you feel like meeting you was the most impressive thing he'd done all day. Now that's a true art.

With this fresh perspective on the baller, I decided to go straight for the jugular. "Would it be possible to interview you for a story for *Newsweek*?" I asked. My friend winced slightly, but I felt we'd made a connection of sorts and the time was right. Without blinking an eye, Jordan offered me the name of his private secretary and told me to call her the next day to set up a time. Being a bit too naïve for my own good, I didn't realize that his quick response could have been from years of being asked the same question every day.

The fact that he could have been giving me the ultimate blow off never crossed my mind until I mentioned to my editors back in New York that I might be getting the story. They understandably had little faith in Jordan's agreeing to a sit-down with me since *Newsweek* had done several covers on the superstar but had never been able to make it through his massive array of representatives to get his participation. It could only be worse now, in the first few months of his return to the court. Every magazine from *GQ* to *Essence* was angling for an interview, and while Jordan was gracious enough to talk at length to reporters after games in the locker room, time for one-on-ones with news organizations was something he couldn't—and wouldn't—spare.

But despite the hundreds of reasons Jordan probably wouldn't talk to me, I made the call to his personal secretary. What did I have to lose? In an act of desperation, I played the race card. I told her that I was one of only a few African American female reporters at the magazine and that an interview with someone like Jordan would greatly help my career. She patiently listened and said she would get back to me as soon as she'd spoken with him.

Somehow I never lost hope, and after a few days, she called back and said that if I came to Chicago and stayed for a week or so, Jordan would find time to speak with me. Bingo! A sports journalism career was born.

I flew back into the Windy City the week after my first

meeting with Jordan. For four days straight, I braved the cold mornings to spend my days in Deerfield, Illinois, where the Bulls had their training facility. If you cover the NBA long enough, you learn the drill that most of the league's teams adhere to, which includes daily morning practices that last about two hours and hour-long shootarounds on game days. Players who want to speak with the media usually do so after either practice or the shootaround. Since Jordan's assistant hadn't been able to give me an exact time for our little chat, I knew I'd just have to be a constant presence at both.

Attending the Bulls' practice was akin to seeing a different film every day. Nut jobs, reporters, and fans alike would line up outside the facility to see Jordan, of course, but there were also Scottie Pippen and the ever-entertaining Dennis Rodman to keep them interested. If the practices weren't entertaining enough, I also attended several games during my wait-and-see-if-Jordan-really-blows-you-off week.

By the time I'd attended the second game of my five-day stay, I was becoming pretty concerned that I was wasting my time and my last good sweater. A drastic decision had to be made. I was going to have to enter the locker room. Up until that point, I'd just leaned against the wall leading into the room where the supertall men were dressing and undressing. I told myself that I didn't want to fight the posse of newspaper reporters who had next-day deadlines on stories about the game itself. But the truth was I didn't want to put myself in an uncomfortable position.

It had become abundantly clear to me that sports journalism was about as male dominated as the sporting events themselves. And the competition among major publications to be first on the story, whatever it was for the week, was as brutal as covering the White House. The mere knowledge that a major national magazine like *Newsweek* was hounding around for a story on Jordan was enough to get the beat reporters second-guessing themselves for weeks on what they'd missed. Up until that night, it had been enough just to get a glance or a nod from Jordan to indicate he knew I was still waiting. But now my editors were calling daily for updates and had pretty much decided it wasn't going to happen. So I had to go in.

Fortunately, when I made it into the locker room that night, there were just a handful of players walking around with towels around their waists. To this day, I continue to be amazed at the number of athletes who don't seem to concern themselves with being completely unclad in a room full of cameras and reporters. But then again, I was one of the very few women allowed into the locker room, especially back in 1996. Today, there is more emphasis on being dressed in NBA team locker rooms because more women have access.

My thought on that first day in the locker room, however, was the more obvious question: Is Jordan going to come out here with just a towel on? The mere idea was going to be a lot for me to handle. After all, I was the only woman in the room, plus I was still pretty intimidated by Jordan's presence in full-on suit. Thankfully, he never came out to meet the media until he was fully dressed in one of his eye-catching suits, a trait Kobe Bryant would later replicate. When Jordan emerged from behind the silver doors where the showers and therapy took place, I was nearly mowed down by members of the press, also knocking one another down to crowd around him in front of his locker.

After I made sure I hadn't been injured in the stampede, I stood back and learned a lesson I would use for years to come in locker rooms across the country—the versatility of a stiletto heel. Stilettos can clear a path in a New York minute, and this sistah, who already had space issues in the midst of too many people, needed to get out of the crowd and gain Jordan's attention. Fast. So I stepped on a few feet. Literally. Okay, the feet of the men who had nearly decapitated me with their wires and microphones in the first place. Yet unlike them, I apologized profusely as I pushed my way through. My heels got me right up in Jordan's face, and all Number 23 could do was laugh when he saw me.

I'm sure his reaction was due to the look of utter desperation on my face. He mouthed, "Tomorrow in Deerfield," without me having to say a word. Thank God I didn't have to explain to the brother that he was putting me in a bad situation.

The next day, true to his word, we sat down on a wooden bench in the practice gym after everyone had left and discussed everything from his love of grape soda and honey buns to his feelings on being away from the game he loved so much while coping with the pain of his father's death. He spoke honestly about how he felt his absence from the game and the Bulls had given the second best player on the team, Scottie Pippen, a taste of what it was like to be in the fire.

"I think Scottie got a chance to see what a leader does,"

said Jordan. "He would have never been able to find that out if I hadn't walked away. It's easy to talk about what a leader could or should do when you aren't one." Jordan's comments seemed a bit harsh, but he and Pippen hadn't had the closest of relationships during Jordan's first Bulls stint. Pippen was a much more mellow guy and did what he could to avoid confrontations.

Jordan, charm notwithstanding, was completely the opposite. He enjoyed nothing better, in fact, than getting in anyone's face with a quickness if he didn't like what he saw on the court. Stories of his many tongue-lashings were like campfire tales to reporters. It also wasn't uncommon to hear the shaken comments from a player after one of Jordan's dress downs. I myself heard Jordan ask his then Bulls teammate Dickey Simpkins, "When are you gonna turn pro?" This question might not have been so brutal and inappropriate had Simpkins not been in the NBA for about three years at that point.

My chat with Jordan went on for about an hour that day and marked the beginning of nearly four years of covering the NBA legend on a near-monthly basis. Thanks to Michael Jordan, I made so many trips to Chicago that I was able to cash in on four frequent-flier trips to Paris.

One day, I decided to get to the arena a couple of hours before a game because I noticed that fans gathered in huge numbers just to get a glimpse of Jordan. Naturally, I wanted to capture those moment for stories, and as a result, I found yet another opportunity to spend uninterrupted quality time with my subject, which helped further my connection to the player and develop even more unique stories.

It was these moments when I met Jordan at his car in the tunnel of the United Center that I learned about his dry sense of humor; his thoughts on his younger sister Jackie's singing aspirations (and how he was so concerned after a major Los Angeles earthquake that he sent a moving truck the next day to bring her back to Illinois); and how generous and loyal he was to longtime friends. On a lighter note, we'd also talk about topics that I knew he had interest in, like Aretha Franklin or Ice Cube, given that *Friday* was his favorite movie.

For *Newsweek*'s purposes, profiles on athletes like Jordan had as much to do with the people they became once off the court as with their ability on the court. But learning the personality of someone like Jordan was not easily accomplished. Savvy and focused, Michael Jordan self-edited a great deal in his conversations, and it was a while before I began to learn how to break through that barrier, even just a little bit. Along with the added one-on-one time meeting him at his car provided me, I was able to see a dose of the reality Jordan went through as probably the most popular person on the planet at the time.

Fans would line up in droves in front of the tunnel where he parked and literally throw themselves in front of his Porsche (or whatever he was driving that day) in an effort to get a smile, a wave of the hand, or in the best-case scenario, an autograph. Tears would stream down their faces at just the glimpse of his bald head and lean frame. To have that degree of fame and worship has to play tricks with even the most stable of minds. Watching Jordan carefully navigate that slippery slope of adoration as an African American man in a mainstream society that often demonizes men who look just like him was a fascinating ride.

The last game I saw Jordan play in person was in the spring of 2003 when the Washington Wizards played the Los Angeles Lakers. Although the Lakers won, nothing could overshadow Jordan's signature calm under pressure. Yet in true Kobe Bryant style, he wouldn't let MJ have his final bow at the Staples Center.

In the first half alone, Bryant scored more than thirty points, rare at the time because he was still supposedly sharing the ball with Shaquille O'Neal. It was clear that Bryant was trying to make a point, perhaps that *he* was "Heir" Jordan. But it was also clear that the crowd was none too pleased with his grandstanding. Even the actor John Cusack, a longtime Jordan fan, audibly booed Bryant. However, Jordan, ever the class act, was in full support of Bryant's performance, saying after the game to reporters, "No matter who's on the court, you have to play your game."

I often think of the period after Jordan left the game for the final time and was attempting to master the skills of general-managing an NBA team in Washington, D.C. The reverence shown to him while he played was nowhere in sight as he fought to find his way on the other side of the court. Jordan struggled with recruiting and draft picks. The Wizards had the number one draft pick in his first year as the team's general manager, and he chose the high school phenom Kwame Brown from Georgia. But Brown was a disappointment from the start because of his lack of maturity on and off the court. As a result, serious questions arose concerning whether Jordan knew how to put a winning team together.

Jordan's impatience with not winning most likely caused a divide between himself and the team's owners, coaches, and players. During this period, I had little to no contact with Michael Jordan because of the tumultuous time he was having in his new role. Indeed, this experience was a failure that was on very public display. I'm not sure Jordan was ready for that reality, but failure or the end of a historically successful career is something many athletes—even the most beloved—must face. Still, Jordan hasn't allowed his past experience to deter him from trying to lead another NBA team, this time in his home state. No doubt it will be interesting to see what his role as part owner of the Charlotte Bobcats will produce. Regardless, Jordan's stake in the North Carolina NBA team in many ways brings his life and career full circle.

Trouble Man

"IRON" MIKE TYSON

When I was growing up, I loved watching sports on television even though I was a self-proclaimed "girly girl." For some reason, my mother insisted on my wearing frilly, short dresses every day of elementary school, which made it practically impossible for me to participate in any school-related sporting event or, at the very least, be taken seriously if I wanted to play. But despite that limitation, my older cousin Bruce and I would watch tennis matches featuring John McEnroe or Björn Borg for hours on end in my grandmother's sun-filled kitchen.

When we were out of school during the summer, we'd often rise before the crack of dawn to see every round of the French Open and Wimbledon. Basketball became my favorite sport to watch while I was in high school, and I now admit I shamelessly rooted for the Detroit Pistons purely because I thought Isiah Thomas was cute. Boxing, however, was never on my list of must-see sporting television. It was too bloody, too brutal, and with the exception of Sugar

Ray Leonard, none of the boxers were much to look at in my opinion.

Still, Mike Tyson was too dominating a figure to ignore. His complicated background, his marriage woes, and his eventual conviction of rape all made frequent front-page news. His unfortunate plight was regularly debated within the African American community, and I often found myself engaged in such a discussion whenever a group of friends got together.

Though I knew the fighter's saga like the back of my hand, I never saw my journalism career veering toward sports until an unexpected opportunity to deal with him came my way in 1995. I'll never forget meeting Tyson for the first time. He was holed up in his Ohio home just days after being released from prison for rape. We'd been introduced via telephone through a mutual friend in Los Angeles, and I made plans to fly to meet him in person that week. I convinced *Newsweek* to let me bring a friend along to avoid any awkwardness. The night we arrived, it was raining cats and dogs, so we checked into a relatively cheap motel a few miles from the airport in Toledo. Though the weather was dreary, I called Tyson's residence, because I didn't want to risk the fighter changing his mind about our meeting.

During our first phone call, Tyson was pleasant but understandably apprehensive as I explained my plans for a story. He hadn't done an interview since being released. Our mutual friend, Alex Avant—the son of the former Motown Records president Clarence Avant—had coaxed the fighter to see me by promising I'd be cool and the piece would be fair. That night Tyson said me and my friend should come on out. It was about nine o'clock, and through darkness and a blinding rainstorm, I navigated the rental car along narrow streets until I found his stately mansion in the middle of Amish country. His friend Craig Boogie let us in through the gates, which featured massive boxing gloves engraved into the steel.

The house was dimly lit and filled with balloons, flowers, and cards, all welcoming the then twenty-nine-year-old fighter home from his four-year stint in prison. A much slimmer Tyson was positioned near the kitchen on a stool with about three pagers and two phones sitting before him on the counter. He was eyeing them all while watching two television monitors that showcased the outside of his home. Since he'd been released the previous week, droves of women had been stopping by at the front gate to leave notes and phone numbers for him. Tyson seemed amused by it all. My friend and I introduced ourselves while he fiddled with his gadgets. He smiled slightly but didn't particularly blow us away with his charm. He offered us a late dinner, which we refused, and then the four of us (Craig Boogie included) settled in front of the television in Tyson's all-wood entertainment room to watch music videos.

Though I'd come for an interview, it was clear that Tyson was in no mood for questions. In retrospect, I think this was his test of me, to see if he liked me enough to bother talking at all. At around eleven o'clock, the fighter suggested we spend the night in one of his mansion's many bedrooms because of the rainstorm. My girlfriend and I nixed that idea without so much as glancing at each other.

He then asked us both to come back the following day for lunch and more conversation. I could only hope that he'd be in a better place the next day, because the person I'd met that night was dark, complex, and somewhat off-putting. This certainly wasn't the profile of Tyson I had hoped to paint. Numerous mutual friends had always described the fighter as gentle, giving, and funny, even while behind bars. That was the Tyson I wanted to reveal to the masses.

Fortunately, the sun was shining brightly the next morning, which gave me a more optimistic view of what the day would bring. We arrived at the mansion around noon, and Tyson himself welcomed us at the door. The difference in his mood was striking—like night and day. He happily took us through his home, which in daylight we could see was not a candidate for *InStyle* magazine. Most of the furniture was unreasonably huge and ornate, with one room—design courtesy of Don King's wife—decorated in wall-to-wall leopard print. It was the most disturbing use of fabric I'd ever seen. We wound up in the kitchen, where his private chef had made us a satisfying lunch. As we ate, Tyson doled out tidbits about life behind bars, his marriage to Robin Givens, and how he stayed hopeful throughout his time in prison. He kept to a strict daily regimen of shadowboxing, jogging, and weight lifting, as well as worked on getting his ego in check. "I was arrogant and still full of myself from my days before, when I did anything I wanted to do and people accepted it," he explained. "I thought I could carry that inside, but an older brother told me I wouldn't make it out alive without a serious change, and he was right."

Then the conversation turned to mummies and how

Tyson had always been fascinated by them and the history of Egypt. Though the shift was a little odd, I used it as an opportunity to connect even further with the fighter. I'd been to the British Museum earlier in the year and mentioned their extensive mummy exhibit. Tyson was riveted by my every detail, and I was mesmerized by his thirst for knowledge.

While in prison he'd read book after book on any number of subjects, and although he didn't always comprehend what he read, he continued to want to know more. He'd read everything from Voltaire and Tolstoy to works by the late black historian Dr. John Henrik Clarke, but he chose to pass on reading a book sent by Dr. Ruth with sex tips. "I don't know why she sent me that," the boxer said, clearly baffled. His mood changed slightly when he told us about the recent death of his older sister. Without much emotion, he also mentioned an older brother, whom he described as "bougie" and that he'd put through medical school. Mike seemed disappointed that he and his brother had virtually no relationship.

As we wrapped up lunch, Tyson invited me to his garage to see the many books he'd received while in prison. Stacked on top of one another in front of his many luxury cars were boxes of books and letters. I was amazed by the numerous pieces from Maya Angelou, John F. Kennedy, Jr., and Spike Lee, to name just a few. Tyson noticed my particular interest in the JKF Jr. letters and explained that the son of the former president had visited him several times in prison and wrote to him often. He said he was one of his true friends.

Without skipping a beat, the fighter offered the letters

and books to me as a gift. "You can have them if you want, since you like him so much," he said. I was stunned. These were at the least collectors' items and, far more important, items the fighter would one day cherish even more. But giving was Mike Tyson's way of operating in a world that had not given him very much in the way of kindness or sympathy. He gave to friends almost to a fault in an effort to make them like him a little more. And though I'd just met the fighter, I could tell he considered me a friend already.

Over the years, I often heard stories of money Tyson had shelled out to women and friends for any number of reasons, and of course, he never got the money back. And while I turned down his offer of the letters and books, more than a few of his friends and associates hadn't been so kind. My friend and I stayed the remainder of the day, listening to his stories of why he'd turned to Islam in prison and how he hoped to regain his fighting shape. Tyson's demeanor throughout the weekend was the worst possible conundrum in terms of my being able to get a good read on him. He loved mummies, for goodness' sake. None of the pieces of the puzzle fit.

After returning to California that Monday, I remembered Tyson telling me about his older brother, who was a pharmacist in Orange County. For two days straight, I called every Tyson, doctor or otherwise, in the phone book in the hope of getting an honest sounding board. Finally, I hit pay dirt when the gentleman on the other end of the line paused as I asked if he was the brother of the fighter. Most others immediately said no with a laugh. This man hesitantly admitted he was indeed Tyson's older brother and listened carefully as I explained how I'd like to talk to him about their childhood and the relationship he now had with his younger brother. He was silent when I finished, so I asked him if he would consider speaking with me. He said he would and hung up abruptly. The next day I called again to see if my plea for an interview was still accepted, but I had to laugh when the number had been changed to an unlisted one.

Although I had no doubt the man I'd met the first night of my stay in Ohio was capable of being an irrational, mean-spirited brute, I'd also seen a likable, troubled soul who'd been abused and taken advantage of nearly his entire life. The final product that appeared in *Newsweek* was not the story I'd envisioned for many reasons that are hard to explain. To be honest, I'm not sure I've ever read a profile that accurately captures Mike Tyson in all his many faces. But our article did give an indication of how conflicted a figure he really was and continues to be.

The next time I saw the fighter was a year later in Las Vegas, where he was preparing to fight again for the first time. He was working out day and night in a little gym on the outskirts of town, so I flew out hoping to see him. As with other subjects I've profiled, I was worried that Tyson might have disliked the piece so much he'd never talk to me again. I found him in the ring sparring with his trainer, and when his handlers gave me drama about getting in the room to say hello, he immediately called out, "Hey, that's my friend." The article seemed the furthest thing from his mind when he jumped out of the ring and gave me a hug. We talked briefly about the upcoming fight and how he was preparing both mentally and physically. He invited me to the megaevent, and I gladly accepted.

I'd recently wanted to experience a Tyson fight firsthand. Friends had described his fights as the most out-of-control fun you could imagine having, and not just for what was happening in the ring. That weekend, a group of friends and I drove to Vegas to see what all the hoopla was about. The fight was being held at the MGM Grand on the strip, and thousands of people had come to the City of Sin just to be in the midst of the action. I was amazed at the number of pimps, hoochies, wannabe rappers, actors, and wayward fight fans who covered the hotel like a bad cologne. Most of them didn't have tickets for the fight, which cost five hundred bucks or more. The fight ended with Tyson winning and everyone's ears left intact.

Later that same year, the fighter invited me and a few friends of mine to his thirtieth birthday party at his home in Connecticut, now owned by the rapper 50 Cent. It was going to be a three-day event with thousands of dollars spent on food, drinks, and entertainment. Most of the guests were being put up in a nearby hotel, and buses transported us each day to the main events. This home, fortunately, had much better decor than his abode in Ohio (although the dance floor, complete with a silver disco ball in the center of the house, was a questionable use of space). I can't remember having as much fun as we did that first night and the rest of the days. From riding motorbikes in his massive backyard during lunch to dancing until the wee hours while Al B. Sure! crooned eighties hits, it was nonstop action.

Tyson beamed with joy as he watched famous friends like Prince, Snoop, and Jamie Foxx spend the weekend wishing him the best of birthdays. Since that year, I've followed Tyson and his career on and off with great interest but even more sadness. The troubled soul I first met on that rainy night had wasted the best years of his career in prison, and the frustration of that, I think, ate away at what little peace he'd found.

Leader of the Pack

EDDIE MURPHY

Back in the high-flying eighties, Eddie Murphy was without doubt the brightest star burning in Hollywood and beyond. Known as the leader of a Hollywood elite posse called the Black Packers, which included Robert Townsend, Arsenio Hall, and Keenan Ivory Wayans, Murphy had a cutting-edge, dead-on take on African American humor that pushed the comedy show *Saturday Night Live* to new heights. Even in the face of the dominant stardom of John Belushi and Chevy Chase, Murphy held his own and shined in silly skits like "Mr. Robinson's Neighborhood" and "Buckwheat."

At the time of Murphy's rise to fame, I was in junior high school, and while I loved the antics of the master comic Richard Pryor, Murphy had an edge that was closer to my age and reality. The fact that this kid from Brooklyn could take Hollywood by storm was fascinating to me. His appearance on *The Tonight Show* was the only thing worthy of my being allowed to stay up past eleven o'clock on a school night.

By the time I'd entered Atlanta University, Murphy's popularity was at its height, as was his massive salary. His brash humor had transferred from television to film quite nicely, with box-office megahits like *Trading Places* and *Beverly Hills Cop*. By the late eighties, the New York native was making nearly $10 million a film and had single-handedly coined the term *posse*. Murphy was notorious for having no fewer than fifteen people with him at all times, which came in handy for the legendary all-night parties at his spacious New Jersey lair known as Bubble Hill.

The stories of his wild shindigs and endless womanizing did little to take Murphy's name off the most eligible bachelor lists of the late eighties. At the time, the NBA had yet to become the dominant source of black men with mega-money, and hip-hop, with its notable salaries and displays of bling, was still in its infancy. Murphy had a thing for dating college girls and spent a great deal of his off time hanging out at historically black colleges and universities, like Howard in Washington, D.C., and Spelman in Atlanta. So it was little surprise that word of his presence on the Atlanta University Center campus spread through the dorms at warp speed. Girls would skip classes to make their way to the Lenox Mall in a mad-dash attempt to purchase something to wear worthy of Mr. Murphy's or any of his buddies' undivided attention. It was quite the scene, with young women sporting elaborate hairstyles and brightly painted makeup, complemented by tight, short, and colorful attire with heels that added another four or five inches of height.

By the time I made it to Los Angeles in the early nineties in my quest to work in entertainment, Murphy had married a former model, and although he was still making films, his star was slowly on the decline. He'd lost the landmark plagiarism lawsuit over his film *Coming to America,* and projects like *The Golden Child* were viewed by Hollywood as box-office bombs because their receipts didn't add up to what had become typical for an Eddie Murphy film blockbuster. But the people he'd put on—Arsenio Hall, Robert Townsend, Keenan Ivory Wayans, and a host of other comics—were benefiting greatly from Murphy's success and his gracious habit of extending help to up-and-coming African American comics.

One infamous story placed a very funny new comic on the receiving end of the star's giving. Murphy provided the struggling performer cash, opportunities to audition for his many films, and a chance to stay in his spacious home in Los Angeles. Unfortunately, the young star got a little confused by his luck and instead stole Murphy's Rolex watch along with a few other things. Despite the comic's amazing gift, Murphy made sure the young man never worked again. *That* was the power of Eddie Murphy, with or without a continuing string of box-office blockbusters.

Although his hits had become fewer, Murphy continued to rule the party scene. Receiving an invitation to one of his parties was like winning the golden ticket for a weekend with Willy Wonka. A plush setting crowded with a who's who of the A list in Hollywood, music, and sports, along with an endless supply of food and drink was just the start of a Murphy party. But Hollywood is an interesting machine, and in the blink of an eye, power can shift. The continued emergence of Murphy followers such as Martin

Lawrence, Chris Rock, Arsenio Hall, and the Wayans Brothers ironically all helped erode Murphy's once strong hold on Tinseltown. Then along came a little film titled *Vampire in Brooklyn,* which sealed Murphy's cinematic coffin with poor box-office receipts and even worse reviews. I actually liked the film, which also starred Angela Bassett, but I, it seemed, was in the minority.

Murphy stepped away from the spotlight for a while and stayed close to home at Bubble Hill with his wife and their growing family. But in 1996, word began to spread that Eddie Murphy was working on a unique project that would feature him as several characters at once. The film was *The Nutty Professor,* and early reviews predicted that it would elevate the onetime cover boy for *Vanity Fair* back to his original heights of stardom.

Murphy was always a sensitive type, despite the hell he gave many a subject during his one-man comedy shows. Remember his hilarious bashing of Bill Cosby? Given how much he could dish it, one might have assumed that Murphy could take it. On the contrary, he was so sensitive that when a friend of mine told him she didn't like his music (during his short-lived recording career), Murphy promptly put her out of his room. So you can imagine what the potential success of *The Nutty Professor* must have meant when he was finding it hard to reestablish momentum in his career.

My gut told me that this film would resurrect Murphy's career, and I wanted to write a piece that would detail his return. But convincing my editors wasn't going to be easy. Even though they'd put him on *Newsweek*'s cover years before, they thought his best days were far behind him. Yet I continued my campaign to get Murphy in the magazine, no matter how small the space given. My editors relented, offering half a page. Not great—but I was desperate.

Unfortunately, convincing Mr. Murphy to cooperate was another problem. His publicist reported that, gun-shy over bad press from his last films, the comic was not eager to speak to a reporter from a major magazine about what his future might hold. He'd said, "I read in *Newsweek* that 'Nutty' is my last chance. What does that mean, exactly? Does that mean that Mike Ovitz is going to meet me at the Hollywood sign and kick my ass if it doesn't do well?"

Indeed, I had my work cut out for me, so I began working the back channels. I'd been told the hip-hop mastermind Russell Simmons was producing the film, and after several phone calls to mutual friends, I secured Simmons's treasured cell phone number. I explained to him what I wanted to do with Murphy and how I thought this piece could kick off a renewed interest in the star, which would of course mean additional revenue for him. Simmons agreed to plead my case with Murphy, but several days went by with no word. Convinced the interview had fallen through the cracks, I was blown away when, at the last minute, Murphy's people called to say he'd comply.

He was in San Francisco filming another movie, so I'd have to travel up from Los Angeles and talk to him between scenes. It was June, so I figured all my cutest summer attire would be just fine for a set visit. However, I'd forgotten the famous Mark Twain saying that the coldest winter he'd ever spent was July in San Francisco. I soon found out June was no different. After a quick trip to the mall to revise my wardrobe, I waited patiently at my hotel for Murphy's assistant to call with my interview time.

Although giddy at the chance of finally talking with Murphy, I was secretly praying the interview would happen late in the afternoon, after the Game Six matchup between the Chicago Bulls and the Seattle SuperSonics for the NBA finals. It was Michael Jordan's first appearance in the finals since his return from retirement, and I didn't want to miss it. Of course, when Murphy's assistant called, the interview was slated for game time. I mentioned this, with no serious thoughts about rescheduling, just making idle conversation.

Wrapped in about nine wool sweaters, I made my way to the docks, where the movie was shooting. Murphy's very sweet assistant met me and escorted me to a trailer on the back of the lot. As we walked and chatted about God knows what, I noticed the trailer we'd entered was beyond huge and equipped with the latest technology. At this point, Murphy's assistant led me to the back of the trailer, where a massive big-screen television was set up and tons of food placed all around. The channel was turned to the NBA pregame, and a masseuse was waiting on the couch.

I was told that Mr. Murphy wanted me to enjoy the game and would join me later for a talk. Now at first I was embarrassed; I hadn't meant for him or his people to think the game was more important than our interview. But his assistant assured me that between him filming his scenes and the drama he'd put me through securing the interview, this was

the least he could do. So while munching on strawberries and cream and enjoying a heavenly massage, I watched Jordan win his fourth championship in perfect bliss.

Like clockwork, as soon as the game ended, Murphy entered the trailer with a pleasant smile and the question of who'd won the game. I was immediately struck by how young he looked in person and how completely serious his face was once the smile was gone. This was not the Eddie Murphy from *Eddie Murphy Raw* or even *Trading Places* and that's the Eddie I'd hoped to meet. Not.

As we settled down and began talking about all that had occurred in his life since he achieved stardom as a teenager, I quickly realized that this would be the best interview I would ever have, bar none. I'd found Murphy at a time in his life when the chips were down and he knew it. However, knowing it and coming to terms with it can often be two separate things—particularly for an actor who'd had the popularity Murphy had enjoyed for an extended period of time.

For the next four hours, I sat mesmerized by Murphy's brutally honest tales of turning down roles, for instance in the megahit *Ghost Busters,* and the regret he felt the moment the film came out. He spoke candidly about doing one too many Beverly Hills Cops films and admitted to doing them for the money in the end. "There was no reason to do the third and fourth ones," he said with a dead serious look. "I could tell they were bad—I read the script. But when you never had money—you always want more, and you're worried you're going to run out."

The comedian then discussed his frustration at having

been the biggest star at Paramount Studios during that time and not even being given the script for the film *Ghost* to read. "I deserved for them to come to me first," said Murphy. "That's how you treat your biggest star. You give him the opportunity to say he's not interested. I would have been interested in doing *Ghost*."

We then journeyed back to his heyday and how he was known for being a big spender and an even bigger party thrower. The stories had made him seem like he was having the time of his life. But Murphy was quick to paint a quite different picture. "First off, I was a kid," he said. "I was eighteen years old when I got on *Saturday Night Live* and had no idea what was in store for me. I just knew I could make people laugh, but overnight I became the biggest thing going with people all over me from everywhere."

Once the money began pouring in, Murphy, who admitted trusting few people for most of his life, made sure only close family members and people he'd known for a long time were in charge of his business affairs. That had turned out to be a bad idea. "I had so many people, people in my family, take advantage of me—my money, everything," he said with distinct sadness in his eyes. "It may have looked like fun, but it wasn't. I was always looking over my shoulders wondering who was doing what to me. You have to remember there wasn't a blueprint for me then. Richard [Pryor] was having his own serious issues back then, so he couldn't really help me, and Cosby wasn't a fan of my work. I was just winging it."

He also spoke of the pain he felt when an African American filmmaker criticized his seeming resistance to using his clout in Hollywood to make changes for the better for

African Americans. "If he'd called me to say those things and we'd talked about it, cool. But to say to the press with no regard to knowing what I was doing was just nuts to me. People never know exactly what you're doing or what you're going through. I didn't come into this business after going to college or anything like that. I didn't know exactly how to do a lot of the things that were expected of me."

As he spoke candidly about the people who had betrayed him over the years, I turned the conversation to his once good friend Arsenio Hall. Everyone in Hollywood knew Murphy had given Hall his break by casting him in the film *Coming to America* and by encouraging Paramount to give the comic a talk show that could compete with the likes of Johnny Carson and David Letterman. *The Arsenio Hall Show* was groundbreaking in its showcasing of minority talent, new and old. To help his friend and to make sure ratings remained at the top, Murphy was a frequent guest, offering Hall a chance to show his viewers what it was like to have one of the most famous people in the world as your best friend. But one guest appearance left Murphy livid and the friendship with Hall in shambles.

During an election year, Murphy appeared and Hall grilled him hard on his voting habits. Hall did this knowing full well, according to Murphy, that Murphy had never voted in his life. I vividly remembered watching this show and how absolutely pissed Murphy had seemed as he tried to refrain from lashing out at his old friend. But Murphy didn't hold back in our interview. "I was like, this nigger is crazy. I gave him this damn show and he embarrasses me like this. . . . I made that nigger—I made him. How I held it together to get through that show, I'll never know."

I knew the comments on Hall wouldn't make it into my piece for *Newsweek*. Complicating matters was that I'd also done several interviews with Hall and found him both charming and smart. But there was a sincere disappointment in Murphy's voice that day which struck me as almost childlike. A deep feeling that one too many friends had stabbed him in the back, and the betrayals had taken the joy out of everything he should have been celebrating in his life.

As we moved to wrap our interview at around eleven o'clock that night, Murphy asked me how big a story *Newsweek* would be doing on him. I was surprised because celebrities rarely ask this question of the reporter. Most have their publicists work out the details of size and placement before an interview is agreed upon, but because Murphy had been so honest with me that night, I decided to be completely honest as well.

I told him that my editors had balked at the notion of doing anything on him at all given the last few years of his career and that I had no idea how much space I'd get. I often think about his response when I see a new star who seems to have Hollywood wrapped around his or her fingers. After pausing for a moment, Murphy looked me straight in the eye and asked, "But don't they remember?"

As corny as it may seem, my heart dropped. Murphy could see that I had no answer—no way to explain how someone as famous, rich, and talented as he could now not even get the promise of a column story in a national magazine.

Murphy called to thank me for the piece, which also surprised me, given that it had not been sugarcoated at all. It told the real story of a career damaged by one too many bad decisions. A week later, I received in the mail an invitation to attend the premiere of *The Nutty Professor*, and I was psyched beyond belief. Everyone in black Hollywood would be there to welcome Murphy back to his proper place at the top.

Unfortunately, it wasn't meant to be for me. A little house party thrown by the recently released O. J. Simpson was more important to my editors. Instead of hobnobbing with Will Smith and Janet Jackson, I was sitting in O.J.'s kitchen listening to him tell me how he'd always supported black people and how he'd date a black woman if he found one he was interested in. Why didn't they just keep him in jail?

The feature ended up getting two full pages. *The Nutty Professor* became a smash hit, making $200 million worldwide, without a doubt because of Murphy's stellar performance. I would see him at another premiere some months later, and while his fortunes had changed significantly since the last time we'd met, the sadness on his face hadn't.

Today, Murphy is divorced and settled back in Los Angeles. I rarely see him out, but I perk up anytime I hear he's involved in a project, particularly a film as high-profile as *Dreamgirls,* costarring Jamie Foxx and Beyoncé Knowles. Though Dave Chappelle, Jamie Foxx, and Chris Rock are the visible faces of humor today, each would tell you that there would be no "them" without the talent and success of Eddie Murphy. Maybe one day just the knowledge of that will be enough to make him smile.

10

America's Favorite Father

BILL COSBY

Though I'd heard it time and time again, I never really understood the old saying that comics, despite their humor, are some of the saddest people walking the face of the earth. I did not fully appreciate what this meant until I met the two most important comic icons of my childhood, Bill Cosby and Eddie Murphy.

I met these men separately, at very different times in their lives and careers. Yet they shared a common and unfortunate bond. Pain. As he had for most people over the age of thirty, Bill Cosby had been a fixture in my household for as long as I can remember watching television. From Fat Albert cartoons to all those silly Jell-O pudding pop commercials, which aired nonstop, Cosby was like your uncle who just happened to have a job in television.

Cosby's appeal extended beyond the children who adored him on TV. For my parents, the films he made with his fellow icon Sidney Poitier usually meant a babysitter for me and a trip to the movies on Friday night for them. *Uptown Saturday Night* and *A Piece of the Action* were just two of the offerings of the early to mid-1970s that show-cased all–African American casts and had both Cosby and Poitier in key decision-making positions, with Poitier as director. The importance of those films and the way they were made didn't resonate with me until years later, when I actually had the chance to sit down with Cosby and talk at length.

Our first meeting couldn't have been under more tragic circumstances. In 1996 I proposed to *Newsweek* a cover with my fellow writer John Leland on the generation gap in the African American community. It would juxtapose old-school values with the increasing dominance of hip-hop ideals. I was asked by the magazine's photo editors to suggest my two ideal cover subjects, people who would convey both youthful *hipness* and older wisdom. My thoughts immediately were of Bill Cosby and Shaquille O'Neal. O'Neal was obvious because he had just released a rap album that went along nicely with his day job as the center for the Los Angeles Lakers. Cosby, by contrast, was the father figure of father figures. This was the man who'd given us the seminal hit *The Cosby Show,* which made us all want to live in a New York City brownstone with our four siblings and ultrarich parents.

Unfortunately, Cosby didn't share our interest in his being the cover person, so Quincy Jones posed with O'Neal instead. But several weeks before the story was due to hit the stands, I was surprised by a phone call at 5:00 A.M. from our New York office. Apparently, there were reports on the wire services of the death of a young man with the last name Cosby, and my editors wanted me to find out if he might be related to Bill.

The call jolted me back briefly to my eventful days in college. I'd studied journalism at the Atlanta University Center during the height of Cosby's campaign to promote black colleges nationwide. *A Different World* was a top 10 television show at the time, and Cosby was putting his money where his mouth was by sending his oldest daughter, Erin, to Spelman College. Erin and I had a few classes together early on, though she rarely came to class and dropped out by our junior year. During my senior year, Cosby's only son, Ennis, enrolled at the all-male Morehouse College, and though I'd never had a chance to interact directly with him, his good looks and pleasant manners were the talk of campus orientation week.

As my mind raced with thoughts of his older sister and of times I remembered seeing Ennis walking around the different AUC campuses, I dialed the number for the actress-director Debbie Allen. Debbie was a longtime Cosby friend and associate, and of course, her sister, Phylicia Rashad had starred with the comic as his wife in both of his family comedy hits. "Yes, it was him," Allen said in a low voice. My stomach dropped with the confirmation, even though I'd known from the moment of the call that morning it had to be Ennis. Cosby was too unique a name for it to be a coincidence. This story would be big news for weeks. It had fame, wealth, and murder—all the makings of headline news—rolled into one.

To complicate matters, I'd made arrangements with Cosby's publicist to visit him on the set the following week in New York. I wanted a chance to meet the Philly native in person with the hope that I could arrange for an interview for some other story down the road. I assumed everything would be canceled because of the family tragedy, so imagine my surprise when I was told to make the trip. Cosby would be returning to work the very next week, just a few days after laying his son to rest on the property behind one of his upstate homes. Years later he would tell me, "Comedy is what I do, and nothing changes that. I like to make people laugh. . . . It was so hard the first few months after Ennis's death because people would look at me with such sad faces. I was used to people seeing me and immediately smiling and laughing."

Grief is a very individual thing, and Cosby seemed not to want to grieve alone. Still, I obviously questioned whether it was the respectful thing to do—to go to New York at that time. My editors convinced me it was. So I flew to New York that next week and headed to the set in Queens where the show was filmed. In speaking with Cosby's personal assistant before leaving Los Angeles, I was told to be at the studio a few hours before the taping was to begin.

The assistant greeted me in the lobby and led me to Cosby's dressing room on the second floor. He was sitting in a La-Z-Boy type chair, smoking a cigar with his feet propped up. Looking vulnerable and tired, his face still bore the overly amusing character he used so often in his commercials and television shows. But the familiar smile did little to mask the subtle, faraway glare in his eyes that spoke louder than any words.

Directly above his head hung a colorful quilt with the words "Hello Friend" stitched into it. The quilt was the focal point of the enormous room, and its freshness made it clear that it was a recent addition. "Hello Friend" had been reported as the phrasing Ennis used whenever he greeted someone. I froze for a moment in the face of all that was going on before me. I hadn't known what to expect, and I'd hoped only to say hello.

As I stood there, I had a flashback to my days covering cops at the *Los Angeles Times* during the early nineties. One of the responsibilities of the cops reporter was to check the reports for accidents and deaths. One morning, after reading a memo about the hit-and-run death of an eighteen-year-old riding his bike, I phoned the home to get a comment. Though it might sound cruel, this was the typical procedure at the paper, and most times, friends and family answered, to give the pertinent information without disturbing the immediate family.

This time a woman's cheery voice answered, and though surprised at her demeanor, I went on to ask if she knew the victim and could give me more information on who he was. The silence on the other end of the line was numbing and only worsened by the subsequent loud scream and drop of the phone. I'd been talking with the victim's mother, who had *not* been previously notified of her son's death.

My clumsy questions had announced the most heart-breaking news. I was shaken to my core at what I'd done, though it wasn't entirely my fault. The hospital should never have released the victim's name to the newspaper with notification still pending. Yet that fact did little to make me feel better that day. The mother's scream and the silence of her indescribable pain haunted me for months. I was taken off the cops beat pretty quickly after the incident. I simply didn't have the stomach for it.

Now, five years later, I was standing in Bill Cosby's dressing room praying that I not ask clumsy questions about his
son. Words were not going to come with ease. Fortunately,
his assistant broke the ice by saying that I was just there to
say hello for my magazine. I followed her lead by telling him
that I attended school with his daughter Erin. A wide smile
spread across Cosby's face at the news, like that of a proud
father seeing one of his kids come home with a good job.

He invited me to sit down, and I accepted. We talked for
ten minutes about school, where I was from, and how I'd
landed at *Newsweek*. Then, would you believe, Erin showed
up, and a reunion of sorts just happened. In the midst of
hugs and catching up, Cosby summoned me back to the
couch by his well-worn reclining chair. He asked if I were
interested in doing an interview right then for my story on
the generational divide. I was stunned, but of course I had
my tape recorder in my purse, so I whipped it out before he
could change his mind.

We talked for nearly thirty minutes about the children he
met when he visited schools in the area to give money for
supplies. "They've stopped teaching music in the schools
today, so of course these kids have no idea what music is—
not real music." He said these words between long puffs of
his Cuban cigar, something he has since given up, seeming
only to take time to inhale before issuing another thought
on the downfall of African American culture.

He then made his famous comment about the Jamie
Foxx film *Booty Call*: "If that's all we can put in the theaters, we should just stop making movies." As one might
expect, Foxx was none too pleased. But by far the most
compelling part of the interview came at the very end. I had

no intention of directly asking about Ennis, even though I knew my editors would hit the ceiling if I didn't. Fortunately, Cosby read my reservations. Without pausing to think, he volunteered, "I know you want to ask about my son, and I want to tell you about him."

I looked down at my notebook as he spoke, not wanting to meet the water welling in his eyes. "Whoever took his life is riding with the devil now. They don't know what they did or what type of person they killed. He was a wonderful kid with a lot of love in his heart. That's who they took from us." I turned the tape off as he stopped speaking and we both sat in silence for a few moments as the words sunk in.

While I waited, I wandered his dressing room, looking closely at the amazing African American artwork ever so neatly placed throughout. Within minutes, show runners came in to give the comic script changes. As Cosby began to leave for a run-through of the changes, he turned to invite me to dinner after the show taped. Could the night get any better?

After the two-hour taping, I returned to his dressing room to find it transformed into an elegant dining room set up for ten people. His daughter and her boyfriend, Phylicia Rashad and her then husband, Ahmad Rashad, and the jazz legend Max Roach were all seated. It was truly a scene from Cosby's TV show, with the conversation flowing easily from politics to music to sports while the soothing sounds of Miles Davis's horn lingered in the background. Soul food made by Cosby's personal chefs filled the china plates, and Cosby kept the night lively with jokes and revelations about his upcoming stand-up material. The mood that night was as peaceful as a Sunday dinner after church.

Back at work the next day, we used Cosby's thirty-minute interview as a Q & A that accompanied the main story on the generational divide. I subsequently spoke with Cosby a number of times on the phone, which of course didn't compare in the least to the fascinating evening shared with his family and friends. During one phone interview to get a quote for a story on fund-raising for African American colleges, Cosby asked if I'd talked with Erin recently. He said that she'd returned to college and graduated. Now she just needed a job.

I laughed at this bit of information (I wouldn't get a job if I were Bill Cosby's daughter either), but he seemed serious as a heart attack. I explained that I wasn't *that* close to his daughter, but if I did see her, I'd certainly congratulate her on graduating. "No, tell her to get a job," he responded. I laughed again and said good-bye. Five minutes later, his assistant called me back with Erin's number and address, along with Mr. Cosby's instructions to call her. I have to be honest. I never made that call. Erin would have cursed me out. *I* would have cursed me out.

In 2003, Cosby was set to release a humor book on eating habits and cleaning up his own health. His publicist phoned with the idea of a cover story on the subject, and I eagerly passed it on to the powers that be in New York. I'd often thought about doing a much longer story on the man who was indeed funny yet had layers of intelligence and strength beneath. Cosby had gotten films made in the seventies, single-handedly turned a declining network around in the eighties, and continued to give millions of dollars to educational funds each year. Social and political changes were issues he took to heart. I was amazed that many in the mainstream press had no knowledge of this side of him. Didn't know, didn't want to know, or didn't care. I couldn't tell.

Though a cover of Cosby was not possible, my editors did agree to an extended story. I flew to New York and called a number I was given when I arrived. Cosby answered in his abrupt way and immediately began talking about his book. I interrupted him to explain that I hadn't flown cross-country to talk over the phone. He loudly gave me his ad-dress and hung up as quickly as he'd answered. All I could do was laugh at this man who clearly thought I was a kid playing grown-up at a magazine.

I wasn't too far from the address he'd given me and ar-rived about thirty minutes later at the massive brownstone. An employee welcomed me into the foyer, which rivaled anything I'd ever seen in a magazine or on television. A long, winding stairway was to the left of the room, and standing in the middle, on the marble floor, was a beauti-fully handcrafted mahogany bust of Ennis. Just beyond the foyer was the great room, and sitting on the couch with bright red pajamas on, was Cosby himself.

He laughed when he saw me and motioned for me to join him in the room. And what a room it was. Oil paintings filled every inch of space on the walls. Some were of Ennis and his father together, and others were of Caucasian sub-jects, seemingly dating back to the Civil War period. I was speechless. Not by the paintings of his son so much as by those of several white families. I didn't ask Cosby about this as we sat down to discuss his book and how his health had suffered in recent years because of blockage in his heart.

We talked about foods he could no longer eat and things his mother had taught him when her health started to fail. During the interview, the phone rang off and on, and Cosby would excuse himself for brief periods. Then one call came that he clearly was looking forward to. A college friend of Ennis was on the line, telling the comic that he'd been accepted to medical school. Cosby's eyes danced as he held the phone to his ear, and then without warning, he put the phone down, darted into the foyer, and stood directly in front of the bust of his dead son. "Ennis, Michael passed on his very first try. Isn't that something? That's a Morehouse man for you. Nothing can stop you." Then he placed a kiss on the bronze forehead.

I watched with amazement and heartbreak at this man who clearly, if given the choice, would give up all his worldly possessions just to have his son back with him. Ennis was the child who had hopes to give back to the community by teaching inner-city children. Before his untimely death, he was a Ph.D. candidate in special education at Columbia University. Ennis had his father's passion for bettering the lives of those around him.

We resumed talking about Cosby's three daughters and grandchildren, which I hadn't realized he had. He then offered to show me the entire brownstone, an offer that I, of course, accepted before all the words were out of his mouth. What a history that home must have had. The sculptures, artwork, and trinkets were from all around the world. As we walked through room after room, I managed to get the courage to ask why he had some portraits of white families from the Civil War period. His answer was incredible to me.

"These are the paintings that slaves painted of the slave owners," Cosby said. "These slaves were masterful artists even back then without training or support." Wow, was all I could say. I'd never pictured slaves being allowed to express creativity. Cosby collected the paintings for years from estate sales and auctions.

As I was still reeling from that piece of information, Cosby led me downstairs to the kitchen and dining room. The highlight of the dining room was a large, colorful mural of a mother and sisters in church, hats and all, covering the back wall. The women seemed vividly alive, with subtle detail in every part of the painting. We then ventured up to a cigar room on the second floor, which was filled with Cuban cigars that Cosby could no longer smoke because of his health.

In other rooms, his honorary degrees from every college imaginable cluttered the wooden walls, along with evidence of his alliance to Omega Psi Phi. As we walked level after level, we talked about the extortion case he was involved in, brought by a woman claiming to be his daughter. This incident had occurred around the same time as the death of his son and no doubt had caused tons more pain for a family already grieving. But the comic was very blunt about his feelings concerning the ordeal. "They thought I was ripe for something like this to happen and that I'd just give in," he said. "They were betting on me wanting it all to go away. But I wasn't going to back down from what I knew wasn't true. She wasn't my daughter."

We continued to chat as I headed to the front door. Cosby wanted to know about Kobe Bryant and whether I thought he was guilty. He also wanted to know my feelings about Condoleezza Rice and how I thought the trial of his son's murderer had turned out. He'd deliberately made sure he was in the courtroom during the last days of the trial. He was intent on the jury seeing him and feeling that someone had to pay for the death of his son.

My article, which ran the week after our meeting, was not the usual puff piece about the comic. In fact, I think he was stunned by the complexity of the story and how it covered all aspects of his career and personality. It also captured a beloved icon in the winter of his life, a winter brought on much too soon because of a tremendous loss. To make the point, the piece was titled "Cosby in Winter."

Cosby did not like the fact that I described him as looking tired and drawn. For several weeks he sent me articles (actually reviews of his shows) that he thought would have been acceptable. But puff pieces were not the real Cosby. The real Cosby is a complicated, slightly angry, and very hurt man whose image over the last few years has taken a real beating. His rant about poor black people bringing down the rest of the race was indeed unfortunate.

But there are no books or shows or public organizations that can make me believe Bill Cosby doesn't truly love black people. An African American man with his background and accomplishments has to be given some benefit of the doubt, particularly given the circumstances of his life over the past few years. Maybe Cosby said some things he shouldn't have. Haven't we all? Those words, no matter how painful and jarring, should not be enough to erase his forty years of influencing, changing, and creating positive images of African Americans on television and beyond. In my eyes, he remains the father figure of my generation.

11

Ballers and Shot Callers

RAY LEWIS, ALLEN IVERSON, AND A-ROD

The line between the worlds of hip-hop and sports has been blurred since David Stern and the NBA began using rap songs to promote upcoming games in their weekly promotions over ten years ago. With athletes releasing rap albums on the regular and artists playing in NBA celebrity games whenever they get the chance, it's often hard to distinguish who's the baller and who should be in the recording studio. Covering both worlds for *Newsweek* gave me a pretty good bird's-eye view of the biggest differences between the two worlds that America, for better or for worse, seems captivated by. Ironically, all these sports have a lot in common. First off, waiting hours on end for an athlete is rare, because the NFL, NBA, and Major League Baseball have strict requirements regarding their players being available to the media. That's helped me avoid six-hour waits in downtown recording studios or never-ending video shoots.

However, athletes have their share of drama, and as a reporter covering them, I have seen my share of it. Of course, nothing comes close to the Lakers, who were a regular soap opera for eight years, but other sports stars also had their moments of shine in the book of "I can't believe that just happened."

Like many people who may have been only casual football fans, I'd never heard of the Baltimore Raven Ray Lewis until he was arrested for allegedly being involved in the stabbing deaths of two acquaintances on January 31, 2000, in Atlanta. Riveted, I watched nonstop as ESPN played the faces and places of the crime over and over. And like most people, I found Lewis to be a fascinating character. He became even more fascinating when he was able to plead to a lesser charge of obstruction of justice and go on to win a Super Bowl.

Of course, as soon as Lewis became a free man, *Newsweek* wanted to be a part of the hunt for the first interview. Though the big sports magazines had a better chance at achieving this goal, I loved a challenge. A few of my friends in Baltimore knew the player, so I headed there in the hope of, at the very least, pleading my own case with the star player. He hadn't spoken at length yet to anybody, so I figured I had as good a chance as anyone else. Unfortunately, while I did get a chance to see Mr. Lewis in action at an array of parties and nightclubs, I didn't have the chance to interview him. He and his people indicated that he wasn't ready to talk, so there wasn't much I could do but wait for another opportunity. That chance came about six months later, when Lewis decided to sponsor a weekend to support his many charities.

I flew to Baltimore on September 7, 2001, and immediately checked into a hotel on the outskirts of the city where many of Lewis's celebrity friends were staying. On Friday,

Lewis had hosted a side-splitting comedy night and party with his friends Morris Chestnut, Duane Martin, and Lisa-Raye in attendance. The next day, I hooked a ride with Chestnut to Lewis's home in the suburbs for my chat with the player. It bears mentioning that Morris Chestnut has always been one of my favorite celebrities for a lot of reasons but mostly because he's one of the nicest guys you could ever meet. I'd met him years ago at a 7-Eleven convenience store in Burbank, California, shortly after he'd made his screen debut in *Boyz n the Hood,* and we'd kept in touch.

Riding up to Lewis's sprawling mansion with Chestnut gave me flashbacks to the days when we frequently hung out in the audience of *The Fresh Prince of Bel-Air* on Monday nights and then ate at Roscoe's House of Chicken' n Waffles after the taping. I learned on our scenic ride from the hotel that Chestnut and Lewis had been good friends for a while, which became even more obvious as Chestnut made himself very much at home in the living room when we arrived. Lewis was upstairs, and one of the female twins who worked for him showed me to him. It was hard to miss the gazillion pairs of shoes in his closets or the mink bedspread that lay across his bed. I wasn't sure where I was going, though, as we walked through his bedroom and into an adjoining restroom.

There Lewis sat, getting his hair braided into cornrows by his stylist and offering me the choice of sitting on the edge of the tub or on the covered toilet for the interview. I chose the toilet because sitting on the edge of a tub can be a wee bit uncomfortable for long periods of time. Despite my discomfort and the fact that Lewis had to tilt his head away from me so the stylist could get the braid just right, we had a pretty good chat about the last year of his life. The Super Bowl win had been surreal. "I can't even describe that moment," Lewis said, shaking his head, much to the braider's chagrin.

He also didn't hold back in discussing the ways some of his friends had turned on him during the toughest of times or the Ravens' front office's unwavering support of him while he was under investigation. Lewis quoted scripture like a southern preacher, which explained the Bible that lay on his bed in plain view. When I asked about the night the murders occurred, Lewis, in a rare comment on the record about that night, simply said, "God would forgive me for any sins." What exactly he meant, I'm not sure. I didn't try to surmise or ask him any more questions about it.

The events that led to the two men being killed weren't exactly cut and dried, and Lewis's plea deal indicated as much. We ended the interview pleasantly, with his head half braided. I left with Chestnut to go back to the hotel. Lewis was throwing a big riverboat party that night, so preparations had to be made. On Sunday, the lot of us attended the game and sat in his private box with his mother and sisters as he played his position with all the gusto a big linebacker with stellar reflexes could.

I flew to New York on Monday, all set to write a great story on a footballer who had seen his life and career flash before him and, almost as quickly, had gotten it all back. But it wasn't meant to be. The next day was Tuesday, September 11, 2001, a day the world changed, and my story on Ray Lewis never saw the light of day.

• • •

From the moment he entered the NBA, Allen Iverson stirred up a lot of noise. His poverty-stricken childhood, coupled with his having been put in jail for a bowling alley scuffle while still a high school star in Virginia, gave good copy to just about every newspaper and magazine across the country for years. I remembered my first year at *Newsweek,* foolishly having tried to contact the then sophomore at Georgetown University for a story I was doing on college players going pro. No one had bothered to tell me that Iverson's then coach John Thompson never allowed his players to talk to the media.

The next year, Iverson did enter the NBA and began playing with the Philadelphia 76ers. The magazine was even more interested in profiling the young star, so I flew to North Carolina to attend the team's training camp in early October. Even though I'd made my desire to interview Iverson known to the team's PR reps, it was clear upon my arrival that they had no particular sway over what he did.

Two days into my stay, he did give me a sit-down, and I found the young man who'd often been described as difficult, thuggish, and a pain to deal with pretty likable. I saw the potential for problems, though. The constant media glare, the unrelenting critics, and his desire to stay connected to friends from his old neighborhood all would get in his way as his career moved on. I watched with amazement as Iverson won Rookie of the Year and even attended a game where he went fearlessly one-on-one with Michael Jordan.

A few years later, word began circulating that Iverson would be releasing a rap album, and my editors were once again interested in the star who'd by that time experienced several more run-ins with the law and even more run-ins with his then coach Larry Brown. The record label Iverson was signed to arranged for me to meet with the rapper-baller, this time at the studio in Philly where he was laying down tracks. In typical hip-hop fashion, the interview didn't take place until around 1:30 A.M. The publicist and a camera crew went along for the ride, which was the best-case scenario, given the drama that would go down as soon as we began the interview.

Since Iverson was far away from the basketball court and his team, he had his usual large group of friends in tow, and they turned out to be a rowdy bunch. In fact, during our interview they remained in the room and continued to talk rather loudly. While this was annoying, I'd done interviews with a lot more going on in the background. But Iverson obviously hadn't. As I waited for him to answer a question I'd just asked, he paused ever so slightly, turned his face to his friends, and let out a slew of profanities that sent chills down my spine: "Motherfucker, don't you see me doing a motherfucking interview! Shut the fuck up, you bitch-a-motherfucker. That's what's wrong with y'all asses. That's why you ain't got shit."

As he let out this stream of invective, the group I'd arrived with were all slowly edging our way to the door, because we had no idea where Iverson's short fuse was going to end. But, fortunately, the posse immediately shut it down, and the rest of the interview went off without a hitch. To complete the story, I also had to do secondary interviews with other players on the team and Coach Larry Brown. Brown was coaching the Olympic team that summer at a training camp in Maui, and since the biggest names in the NBA were going to be in attendance, the magazine approved my trip to see them in action.

I had no idea if Brown would want to talk about his most controversial player in his downtime. The two had a true love-hate relationship, with hate being the stronger of the emotions for most of their time together. Surprisingly enough, Brown was more than eager to discuss the thorn in his side, even going so far as to say his wife had told him that Allen would be the death of him. Too bad she didn't have a crystal ball to see Brown coach the Knicks in later years. Brown spoke candidly about Iverson's regular habit of arriving to practice late, his constant eating of Taco Bell and other junk food, and his absolute refusal to lift weights to get his body fit enough to fight off bulkier competitors.

Iverson's teammates weren't shy either with their frustrations, though they requested that their comments be off the record. One of his teammates gave a quote that I'm sure to this day stings Iverson's ears. The longtime teammate referred to Iverson's impoverished background, lack of a father in the home, and overall work ethic. "I grew up without shit and no daddy, but I know how to come to work on time," he declared. Then he continued, "Half the brothers grew up in so-called hard lives, and we're doing what we're supposed to . . . we bring our asses to work on time. It's a bullshit excuse." It was a tough quote to hear and an even more difficult quote to write, but it was a real emotion of a real player. Needless to say, Iverson was not pleased with the article that ran in *Newsweek*. The next time I saw him was at a Lakers game a few months later. I made a point of going in the opposite direction. I'd heard his tongue-lashing before.

While it's hard to deny my lifetime love for basketball, other sports do compete for my attention from time to time. Football has always been my second love—to watch, that is. Being in the locker room definitely isn't one of my favorite pastimes. While covering the Super Bowl–winning Denver Broncos in the late nineties, controversial linebacker Bill Romanowski picked me up by my shoulders and moved me from one side of his locker to another, just so he could walk by. At the time, I was waiting for a quote from John Elway, but given Romanowski's penchant for spitting on people, I decided to keep quiet and skip the protest. Yet, as intimidating as the size and gall of the guys in football, even worse is the horrible smell of the locker room once the game is over. The mixture of pure sweat, dirt, grass, and who knows what else, produces an odor I wouldn't wish to send through my worst enemy's nasal passages. Despite those negatives, I still enjoy the game and love nothing more than Super Bowl Sunday. Damn those Minnesota Vikings for losing the NFC Championship Game in 2000 against the New York Giants!

However, the same cannot be said of my relationship with baseball. Since watching the game is something akin to watching paint dry for me, I never developed a taste for it. But after a visit to the Bahamas one winter in 2000 and laying eyes on the Adonis of a man nicknamed A-Rod, I temporarily changed my mind. A friend and I headed to the Atlantis Resort on a whim for the New Year's celebration, which is quite massive. Atlantis was, and is, the favorite spot of more than a few athletes, and the holidays proved the perfect time for them to converge. Michael Jordan, Tiger Woods, Charles Barkley, and Gary Sheffield were all holed up at the luxury resort for rest and relaxation. Jordan even has a $25,000 per night suite named after him, though I doubt if he ever sees the inside of it. The legend lives at the blackjack table. I'll never forget him sitting at the table from first thing in the morning until late in the night, without seeming to move an inch. The first morning of our stay, my girlfriend and I stopped by to speak to "His Airness," and he even offered us a few of the chips he'd won. I, as a journalist, couldn't accept. Darn!

On the second day of our trip, we stopped by the table again, though this time Jordan was joined by an unfamiliar face. I should note that the face was unfamiliar to me because any self-respecting sports fan would know Alex Rodriguez when they saw him. Anyone, that is, but me. Dressed in a leather jacket, white T-shirt, and jeans (it's chilly in the Bahamas in December), A-Rod was just chilling and enjoying Jordan's finesse at the table as he gambled with a small fortune. He may have thought that by sitting close enough to Jordan, it just might imbue him with the power and strength the legend had displayed during his entire career. A-Rod was in dire need of both, due to the crossroads he was facing in his career at that time.

Before wearing a New York Yankees uniform, A-Rod had left the Seattle Mariners for the Texas Rangers in a blockbuster deal that caused a major backlash for him. The commentary was undoubtedly harsh. From other players in the league, to team owners and president/CEOs, such as Larry Lucchino, to the everyday man and woman on the street, a negative stream of shock and awe prevailed as A-Rod prepared to join the Rangers. For those who don't know the back story, A-Rod, then twenty-five years old, departed Seattle for more money (much more money—a $252 million dollar, ten-year deal to be exact) and headed to Texas, despite the fact that the Rangers were a considerably less talented team. Is there anything fans hate worse? Well maybe. An increase in concession stand and ticket prices doesn't go over too well either.

Back to the blackjack table. Jordan introduced the slugger to me and explained his importance in the game. Jordan could tell I didn't have a damn clue. Although I didn't know A-Rod and what he meant to baseball, he was quite a sight to behold, so I listened intently to every word, temporarily vacating my "baseball is like watching paint dry" opinion. Ironically, during our conversation, A-Rod told me he has long been compared to Michael Jordan by Latino baseball fans. "I've been Michael Jordan in Latin countries for years. . . . I know what I mean to all Latinos and what this game means to them. Baseball is in their blood." Fascinated by his story (and his good looks), I asked A-Rod a bunch of questions which culminated in me inviting myself, I think, to spring training in Florida to watch him play.

It's important to note that spring training for baseball is

another thing all together in journalism. Away from the glitz, glamour, and distractions of the big city, spring training is typically held in a backwoods Florida town called Port Charlotte so the players can focus on the upcoming season. I arrived in late February, excited about a new challenge and what it would bring to my growing sports résumé. As usual, I had no idea what I was walking into. For the first two days, I attended batting practices in which I saw A-Rod come to bat *twice* (twice!) in a four-hour period. Needless to say, I was hot (as in not happy).

The next day, I was more prepared and bought nearly every magazine in the hotel lobby to occupy my blinding boredom, but it didn't help much. The challenging part was that I didn't really have an official contact for A-Rod, just his word that he'd talk to me. Thankfully, this proved not to be a problem when he saw me sitting in the bleachers reading *Vogue* and barely looking at who was up at bat. I walked to the cage to reintroduce myself, and we arranged to talk the next morning before batting practice began at the undesirable hour of 8 A.M. Remember, I was still on West Coast time. I also figured it would be smooth sailing in a baseball locker room. By then, I was a veteran of sorts, having been in several football and basketball locker rooms and surviving Mike Tyson, BE and AE (before the Holyfield ear and after). So how bad could it really be? As it turned out— pretty bad.

When I mentioned women were few and far between in other sports locker rooms, it was the ultimate understatement in baseball. I don't think groupies were even allowed within a thousand feet of the locker room. Still, I was undeterred. I walked into the spacious room with my confidence and no-nonsense stare focused on my mission. It didn't last long because the moment my foot hit the inside of the locker room, the entire room came to an abrupt halt. I was sure I had left the rollers in my hair, forgotten a shoe, or worse—no lip gloss—but it turned out to be the norm. Women were rarely, if ever, seen in a baseball locker room at the time. With a feeling of such uneasiness, I quietly backed out and pulled the ball boy aside to ask if A-Rod was there. He ventured in and returned with the info I needed. A-Rod was eating breakfast in the cafeteria—a public space where women weren't quite so alien. I immediately felt a wave of relief that I was on my way to get the story I came for. What is it that they say in baseball when a player successfully gets to where they're supposed to be? SAFE! No need to return to the locker room of doom.

A-Rod seemed to have been expecting me sooner and looked mockingly at his watch as I approached the table. Over oatmeal and orange juice, I grilled the slugger on everything from what he expected when he returned to Seattle to play on an opposing team to his friendship with Derek Jeter. A-Rod's answers weren't particularly mind-blowing, but were good enough to do the one-page story I'd planned. He sensed that I was wrapping things up and suggested I sit with him outside as he signed a few autographs. I think he wanted me to see that he still had fans despite his sudden move to another city.

I sat beside him at a table as fan after fan walked up with baseballs, pieces of paper, and jerseys for him to sign. Midway through, he turned to me and asked, "Do you know what I find frustrating sometimes?" I wanted to respond, "Boring interviews and hot-ass summer days," but I refrained. Then he mumbled, while looking straight ahead, "It frustrates me that Hispanic reporters want Hispanic baseball players to always speak in Spanish and get mad if they don't." I had to think for a minute about what A-Rod was saying, since I'd only just realized that baseball was filled with a majority of Hispanic players. I understood how this expectation might pose its own set of issues for players, just as it did in the NBA for African American players who saw an endless stream of nonblack reporters asking about growing up in the 'hood.

For A-Rod, who was born in New York and considered English his first language, the burden of being required to speak Spanish to the media and treated negatively if he chose not to, does seem a bit unfair. After all, his choosing not to speak Spanish to the media does not indicate that he's rejecting or ashamed of his Hispanic roots or heritage, it just implies that his preference is to speak English in those instances. Truthfully, I didn't know how to respond. Sensing my apprehension, he bit his lip and asked if I thought his words would offend the Hispanic community. I tried to be as polite as I could when I told him that I had no idea if his words would be offensive. He nodded his head as if to say, "Yeah right" and turned to sign the next piece of paper for an eagerly awaiting fan.

12

Creepin' On Ah Come Up

JODECI'S DEVANTE SWING, TYRA BANKS, BONE
THUGS-N-HARMONY, LIL' KIM, AND EMINEM

As you can imagine, there have been times over the years when I would join a celebrity in a quest to complete some personal business while I did an interview. During the glory days of the R & B group Jodeci, I met up with the pioneering hip-hop-soul group's front man, DeVante Swing, to discuss their album *The Show, The After Party, The Hotel*. A wonderfully talented producer and writer, DeVante had all the makings to become the next Babyface, with his soulfully explicit lyrics and powerfully seductive grooves.

We met on a Saturday morning in the posh lobby of his hotel in Beverly Hills. I was shocked that he came downstairs wearing a clear plastic shower cap, but I was more stunned that he wanted us to walk together through Beverly Hills while he still had it on. To further complicate matters, the Olympic medalist figure skater Nancy Kerrigan happened to be in the lobby at the same time. DeVante, seeing no need to be subtle, turned to me and asked as loudly as he

could, "Ain't that the bitch that got her leg beat?" The hor-
rified look on my face must have answered the question; I
had no words.

Unfazed by the moment, DeVante explained that he
wanted me to walk with him a few blocks from the hotel to
a tattoo salon. It seemed the producer wanted to get an
inked image of the group's new album cover on his arm,
and no interview with *Newsweek* was going to delay it. As
we strolled past luxury antiques shops, ultrahigh-end fashion boutiques, and upscale grocers along Doheny and Robertson, the looks we got from people who had no idea and
didn't care who DeVante was, were priceless, as was his
complete lack of awareness that a shower cap outside the
shower wasn't normal attire.

Still, as we entered the tattoo shop, it was clear that
DeVante was a valued customer, and provisions were made
to begin working on him immediately. Unsure about how
I'd do an interview in the presence of the odor of burning
flesh, I pulled my chair as close as I could to DeVante's while
he instructed the artist on what he wanted. He desired an
outline of a very shapely woman with the title of the new
album running through her waist.

With that taken care of, we got around to the interview.
Despite the obvious pain he was enduring, DeVante was
quite colorful in his answers and displayed an impressive
knowledge of music, both past and present. As the conversation sailed on for more than an hour, it occurred to the hit
producer to check out the work being done on his arm. Our
conversation had been a pleasant distraction until he saw
the nearly finished results.

The artist had indeed grafted the image of a shapely

woman on his arm, but with one hitch. The woman's straight hair hung down past her waist. Upon seeing this, DeVante exploded with the most energy he'd shown all day. "That woman looks white, with all that hair on her head! Why did you put a white woman on my arm?" Seeing that this wasn't going to have a very nice ending, I bade farewell to Mr. Swing, his shower cap, and his white woman, and headed to Neiman Marcus.

Thinking little could compete with a shower cap in broad daylight on Robertson Boulevard in Beverly Hills, lunch with the TV host and supermodel Tyra Banks came amazingly close. I was set to interview the gorgeous diva in 2005, on the heels of the success of her show *America's Next Top Model*. The reality show had been a surprise hit and had transitioned Banks from runway superstar to TV icon and no-nonsense businesswoman to boot.

Being the down-to-earth woman that she is, Banks arranged for us to meet at the well-known Roscoe's House of Chicken' n Waffles in Hollywood for a nice extrafattening lunch. For anyone who doesn't know, Roscoe's is a Los Angeles staple for their wonderfully odd mixture of breakfast food and dinner fare, served day and night. Their golden waffles make the mouth water, and with an added side of chicken with gravy, you might not want to slap your mama (because, in truth, who really wants to do that?), but you will want to slap somebody. Needless to say, I was very appreciative that Banks put her supermodel diet on hold to accommodate my carbs intake for our interview.

I arrived a little early at the eatery, which can be best

described as a scrumptious hole in the wall, big enough to fit only about seventy-five people, with dark pinewood paneling, giving it nighttime appeal in the middle of the day. Fine dining it ain't. I requested a table close to the back for privacy and prepared myself for what I was sure would be a great afternoon. Banks arrived on time and looked wonderful, wearing little to no makeup, a long hockey jersey, and black leggings. Her reddish hair was hidden under a baseball cap, and to my surprise, she was no stick figure. I quickly began to understand her womanly shape as she ordered a hearty meal of waffles, bacon, grits, and eggs. I tried to match her order, but it's mighty hard to savor waffles and ask questions at the same time. Try it if you don't believe me.

As funny as Banks's Hungry Man order was, our lovely waitress beat it by a mile. Banks had managed to walk into Roscoe's with little recognition from the other patrons, and given our secluded table, I was sure we'd have few interruptions. *Not!* As our round-the-way-girl waitress began writing down our orders, she glanced up and loudly announced, "You look just like Tyra Banks!" To which Banks happily replied, "I get that all the time, girl!" For the moment, it was enough to send our observation-happy waitress on her way to the kitchen. But what also makes Roscoe's so amazing is that no order takes more than five minutes to prepare. So before I could get one entire question out of my mouth, our waitress was back at the table with steaming food and a comment I shall not forget as long as I own a tape recorder: "Girl, you *are* Tyra Banks! Your forehead ain't that big in person. You should tell them people at Victoria's Secret to

do something about that 'cause it looks huge in those pictures and on TV."

Yes, sistah girl said it, and all I could do was lower my
head in shame and pain, because I just knew my interview
was dead on the spot. I couldn't imagine any true self-
adoring starlet suffering such an insult without it affecting
her mood in quite an unpleasant way. But you can't judge a
book by its cover, and Tyra Banks is a young woman full of
supreme confidence and surprises. Without blinking an eye
or stopping to catch her breath, she flipped the script by
asking the waitress, "Girl, what should I tell them to do to
make me look better? Let me know your tips." Now, not to
be mean, but our waitress was not someone who needed
to be passing on beauty tips, but you gotta love a sistah for
saying what was on her mind, and you gotta love another
sistah for taking it all in stride.

With that comedy show behind us, Banks and I managed to discuss her exploding success. From her regular vocal lessons in preparation for jump-starting a singing career
to her desire to be the next Oprah "with bigger breasts,"
Banks's ambition was truly inspirational. However, in between tales of her then boyfriend, the NBA star Chris Web-
ber, making her tapes of *The Dave Chappelle Show* to
watch before bed, we had another visitor to our now not-
so-private table.

This time it was a five-foot-four, 175-pound (give or
take) female patron who was interested not in an autograph
but in finding out if she had what it took to be on Banks's
reality show. Banks pleasantly wrote down audition times
and places and told the young lady to keep up her positive

attitude. I was certainly impressed by Banks's graciousness. With her fame and success, it would have been easy for her to dismiss those two women without a thought. Although the interruptions distracted me, they gave me just the right take on a woman destined for an even brighter future than she'd already enjoyed as one of the world's most famous supermodels.

I had a few rules of thumb I always employed when I interviewed anyone of note in the hip-hop community. These were needed for several reasons, particularly since time, or rather being on time, was not the top priority for most of the artists in the bling-bling generation. I once waited six hours for Bobby Brown to show up at a Hollywood recording studio. I know that probably doesn't sound too crazy, given Mr. Brown's and his wife's oftentimes peculiar behavior, but trust me when I say that Bobby Brown wasn't the only famous name who left this reporter hanging for hours on end.

More to the point, I never would have survived those hours without my emergency survival kit: a couple of magazines or one very good book; three bottles of cold spring water; a fully charged phone; and plenty of snacks in case I got hungry while waiting on said hip-hop star, or even better, if the hip-hop star just happened to bring along one of his or her children.

One July morning in 1998, I met up with the members of the group Bone Thugs-N-Harmony in their hometown of Cleveland to watch them film a video for a single from their album *The Art of War*. Besides the fact that they all were adorably cute, to me anyway, their singsong version of a rap tune was so unique to the music landscape at the time that I knew I had to do a piece.

After a short sightseeing tour of the city, I arrived at the shoot location only to realize that it was outdoors by the very cold lakefront. For nearly an hour, I bugged the film crew until Layzie Bone, Bizzy Bone, and one other Bone arrived to get ready for makeup and wardrobe. Another member had been delayed overnight by an arrest that no one felt very chatty about.

Since Layzie Bone had always been my favorite member of the group, I immediately focused on him to steer the direction of the article. Layzie, being a nice guy, had given me his thick jacket to wear as soon as we met. To my amazement, when I put my hand in the jacket pocket, a fistful of hundred-dollar bills fell out. For the briefest of moments, visions of all the Gucci bags I could buy danced in my head, but something about the deep-set eyes of Layzie Bone told me I'd live to regret that decision. So I picked up the wad of cash and put it back in the pocket ever so neatly.

Layzie Bone had also brought along a guest—his then three-year-old, aptly named, and equally adorable son Lil' Layzie. Already quite the Mini-Me, Lil' Layzie seemed right at home among the cameras, wires, and other equipment. Having been a bystander on a number of video sets waiting to interview artists, I quickly became bored and decided to occupy my time following the independent little boy as he made himself a sweet nuisance all over the set. Lil' Layzie was in his own little world, but unfortunately without much supervision. A few times I motioned to his father and his father's publicist that the little boy was getting dangerously close to the water. But Big Layzie only flashed me a smile and said, "Lil' Man can take care of himself."

As much as I wanted to trust Big Layzie's parental wisdom on the ability of a three-year-old "to take care of himself" around a large body of water, I didn't see the upside of having to write about a child nearly drowning while I was attempting to do a story. So I followed this child I'd never met before, hoping he'd listen to a woman who was supposed to be paying attention to his father and not to him.

As I neared the edge of the water, where he was mindlessly skimming his feet, I called out, "Lil' Layzie, don't you want some Skittles?" I always had a bag of Skittles on hand for myself, and fortunately, Lil' Layzie liked them, too. He dashed from the water's edge and snatched the bag right out of my hand with a sly smile. With the other hand, I pulled him back toward the video set as he chose to share with me the number of times the police had been to his home over the last few weeks. In the meantime, not one Bone seemed to notice the adventure I'd just been on with Lil' Layzie. And why would they? Lil' Layzie—or Lil' Man—"could take care of himself."

Shower caps, "round-the-way" waitresses, and wandering sons aren't the only things that can present messy situations with celebs. In 2000 I had the opportunity to interview Kimberly Jones, a.k.a. Lil' Kim, when she was celebrating her new album, which came following a long break after the murder of her mentor and lover Biggie Wallace.

While Kim had been a fixture on the hip-hop scene for quite awhile, I hadn't really pushed to sit down with her until her second solo album, *Notorious K.I.M.*, was about to be released. Through the years I'd done so much writing on the Biggie-Tupac feud and the many loves of Biggie that it almost felt like I'd talked to Kim without ever meeting her face-to-face.

This time, it would be up close and personal on the set of her video in Los Angeles for her single "No Matter What They Say," which would include cameos by her good friends Mary J. Blige and Missy Elliott. This was going to be fun. Interviewing Blige was always a hoot for me. Mary J. and I, even during the worst of her drug problems, always got on well. She never presented anything but a real woman with immense talent and the demons we all have. Unfortunately, her demons played out on a worldwide stage.

When I arrived on set, I was led immediately to the trailer where Kim and the girls were getting ready. Mary and I embraced, and I complimented her on the weight she'd lost. She looked amazing. I'd never met Missy Elliott before, but she was quite pleasant. With Michael Jackson's *Thriller* loudly playing in the background and plenty of banana schnapps to go around, I felt like we were all back in high school and enjoying good girlfriend company. Weight loss, men, black women hair issues, and the newest MAC makeup products were discussed at a far more productive level than was Kim's new album. In fact, by the time the camera crew was ready for them, the singers were falling down the steps they were so drunk. It was a funny moment, especially since it was only noon.

What is not so funny is when I think about the fact that,

although Kim's journey into plastic surgery hell had already begun by the time I'd interviewed her, it wasn't nearly as dramatic as it would turn out to be. I recall watching while she prepared for an awards show in Las Vegas. I had arranged to hook up with her in her hotel room, where she was getting dolled up in an "almost dress."

A ton of people were going in and coming out of the room that day. Kim's before-the-snitching pal Lil' Cease walked in all smiles and full of compliments. Another former member of Kim's crew had some goodies that he offered to everyone in sight, including me. Cocaine. As one might imagine, it wasn't often that I was offered cocaine. Geez, Snoop Dogg never offered to share his weed with me the dozen or so times we hung out. Although I was flattered by the gesture, I politely declined.

I made myself at home on a couch and watched Kim's makeup artist attempt to make every African American–like feature on her face disappear. To be clear, I'm not judging Kim. Show business is brutal, and even more so for an African American woman with non-European features. In fact, I wrote in my *Newsweek* feature "A Whole Lotta Lil' Kim" Kim's thoughts on why she'd transformed herself from girl in the 'hood into blue-eyed blonde. "I have low self-esteem and I always have," she said at the time. "Guys always cheated on me with women who were European looking. You know, the long-hair type. Really beautiful women that left me thinking, 'How can I compete with that?' Being a regular black girl wasn't good enough."

She also vividly described the pain she suffered while getting breast implants ("That surgery was the most pain I've ever been in in my life") and what it was like to be discarded by the Notorious B.I.G. once he became famous. Her blinding love for the rapper was sort of endearing but also difficult to digest, given the amount of agony he seemed to have caused her. Yet at the time she still kept some of his ashes in an urn at her home in New Jersey.

I last interviewed Kim in 2005 just days before she was due to start serving her prison sentence after being convicted of lying to a federal grand jury about a gun battle outside a hip-hop radio station in New York City. I met a different Kim this time; she was more mature and toned down, more fashionably dressed than undressed. She'd also had more plastic surgery, and it wasn't a pretty sight. Her nose was razor thin, and her skin was considerably lighter. I'd hoped she'd found more peace in the years since we'd first met, but peace with your inner self is a hard thing to come by it seems. There were still people around her, mostly close friends and associates, and there was even a camera crew following her for what would become the hit BET reality show *Lil' Kim: Countdown to Lockdown*.

Yet, in the midst of all the conversation and excitement, Kim was a portrait of quiet and contemplation. She obviously had plenty on her mind. "I had a lot of offers for movies and television before this all happened," she said. "And all I can pray for is that they will still be there when this is over. They will if it's meant to be." All signs thus far indicate that it is indeed meant to be.

Unfortunately, the sad tale of Lil' Kim isn't the only unpleasant ending for a rapper with whom I once had a chance to spend time. In late 1999, I accompanied Dr. Dre and

Snoop Dogg to Hawaii for a concert they were doing as a part of a local radio station contest. I was doing a rather large profile on Dr. Dre, and since I'd done about a dozen profiles on him before, I needed a new scene for the lead.

The trip started off with a bang since Suge Knight had sent some of his rough and tough boys on the trip as well, a routine scare measure he used to keep Dre and Snoop on the lookout for trouble. This tactic didn't prevent Dre from enjoying the sun and fun of the island, but Snoop decided he'd keep his appearances to a minimum that weekend. On the night I arrived (naturally, on the same plane as some of Suge's boys), Dre hosted a dinner at a small restaurant just a few miles from our hotel.

The intimate affair was held in the back room of an Italian eatery and included a security guard just outside the room. I was really saddened that Dre had to take such precautions to live a normal life, but it didn't seem to hold him back a bit. Guests included key people from his label, Interscope Records, Dre's wife, Nicole, and an attendee I hadn't expected—the red-hot rapper Eminem.

At this point, the Detroit native was early in his success, and it showed in his relaxed demeanor. The night was filled with endless jokes—Dre has quite the sense of humor—and Eminem was a good match, actually ordering, "All the white people leave the room." Of course, he didn't budge. He was gleefully enjoying himself and his newfound megawatt fame. The night ended well after midnight, with Eminem purchasing red roses for all the women at the table. He was on top of the world, and while that was the only time I had the opportunity to be around the rapper, I watched with amazement as his domination of the rap game continued.

If I've learned one thing about this business, it's that nothing is ever as good as it seems. I often think of that night when I read the sad tabloid stories about the man who mesmerized the country with each of his albums. Stories of Eminem's prescription drug addiction and abuse; his on-again, off-again marriage to his longtime love, Kim; and the death of his best friend let me know that the innocence I once saw in a young man who'd achieved everything he'd ever dreamed of had all but disappeared. I've also learned that dreams can come true, but so can nightmares. I'm not sure whether Eminem would characterize his life as a dream or a nightmare at this point, but do I know too much of a good thing can result in exactly the opposite.

On Lockdown

SUGE KNIGHT AND MALCOLM SHABAZZ
IN PRISON

Spending time in, visiting, or going to a prison for any reason has never topped my list of things to do. But given some of the infamous subjects I've chosen to cover over the last twelve years at *Newsweek,* I didn't have much of a chance of staying outside the concrete walls for long. The person who made sure I had several visits to a number of holding cells was the Death Row cofounder Suge Knight.

I made my first trip to see the embattled music man in the late nineties, after he'd been convicted of violating his probation during the Las Vegas fight that eventually led to the death of Tupac Shakur. Years before, the magazine had run one of the first major profiles of Knight, and I'd continued to follow him and his career.

At first I was worried that a request to visit the rap mogul in prison would be turned down flat by his representatives. Our coverage of Tupac's murder and who might have been responsible for it hadn't been appreciated very much by Knight or Death Row Records, but with time Knight seemed to forgive and forget. I still had friends at Death Row, and they agreed to put me on a "friends and family" list, saying that this would make my entrée quicker. Nevertheless, it still was a long process—six months to check out my name, background, and criminal past, or lack thereof.

Finally a date came down for the interview, and I arranged to make the journey with the PR reps Knight had hired. I'd never been to a prison before, didn't know anyone else who had, or anyone who was on lockdown, so the required attire wasn't exactly on my fashion radar. Rest assured that I made all the wrong fashion choices for my journey up north, but you live and learn—even when it comes to jailhouse couture.

The prison to which Knight had been sent was in San Luis Obispo, a quaint college-type town with a small airport and limited shopping. It was only about thirty minutes by air from Los Angeles, so I boarded the commuter-size plane wearing a very cute running suit. Not one member of his PR team, who I assumed were fully aware of the dress code, bothered to tell me just how inappropriately I was dressed and how there was no way I'd get into the prison with that getup on.

Oblivious in my all-white Nike tracksuit, I strolled into the San Luis Obispo prison ready to see the man who'd helped give me a leg up on hip-hop journalism. But the bubble burst as soon as I reached the front desk. A full-on search would have to be done by a female guard, and while I could get away with taking off my running suit jacket, (I had a white shirt under it), I wasn't going to get away with wearing the one thing that truly never crossed my mind as problematic—my underwire bra.

From what I gathered, the logic was that a woman can reach under her shirt, take the wire out of the bra, and hand it over to the prisoner with no one being the wiser. Then, of course, the prisoner could use the wire as a weapon of some sort. This was a dilemma I had no answer for—though I did go into the bathroom to try to rip the wire out of my bra, to no avail. I'm not sure what woman had successfully accomplished getting the wire out of her bra to hand over but she must have had superhuman strength. Every woman knows the only thing that can destroy a good bra is the washing machine.

The prison, however, had their own answer for my problem, which they clearly encountered regularly. They could give me a used bra, sans underwire, courtesy of a collection they kept at the wives and family house in the prison yard. After a quick look at the well-worn collection of bras, which were not so nicely placed in a brown moving box, I decided to be a bra snob and make the trip back downtown to the Victoria's Secret I'd seen while driving through. It would cut an hour from the interview, but it was either buy a new bra or have my skin crawl the entire time while I wondered who had worn the bra before me.

After that minor drama, I got to see Mr. Knight in the family receiving room, and he seemed overjoyed for a visit. For the next three hours, he dazzled me with tales of undercover government intentions to bring him down, record industry executives' reasons for wanting him behind bars, and a little gossip about who was and was not gay. His list went on forever, and for some reason, I didn't have the heart to tell him that not only would his crazy theory about Michael Jordan being gay not go into my story but it was probably the most ridiculous thing I'd ever heard. But calling Suge Knight ridiculous to his face didn't seem the brightest idea, so I just smiled and listened. I could tell that he was enjoying hearing himself talk and that I just happened to be the lucky soul there to hear it.

I would make another visit to Knight a year later, and fortunately I'd made a point of collecting appropriate bras for just such an occasion. This time, what I wasn't ready for was having the singer Michel'e (whom Knight was either dating or married to depending on who you asked) join us for the interview. For six hours I endured her high-pitched, air-being-let-out-of-a-balloon voice as she contributed to the conversation. Meanwhile, Knight continued his who's gay in Hollywood routine, and I continued my pretend-to-care routine as the list became longer and more absurd.

After the interview, I arranged to meet Knight's parents and visit the home where he grew up, in the Compton section of Los Angeles. They couldn't have been sweeter, straight down-home southern folks who loved their son and didn't understand why people felt the way they did about him.

Before the story ran, Knight made numerous calls to me to clarify statements about his former business partners at Interscope Records. Trust me when I say there's nothing like receiving a collect call from a prisoner on a daily basis and then being reminded every thirty seconds with the static recording that you are indeed talking to a prison. It was a good experience for me, as I learned quite a lot about the legal system, not to mention the added benefit of expanding my underwear collection.

After Suge Knight, I hoped that I wouldn't have many more opportunities to make a visit to prison, but all that changed when I heard an interview with the grandson of Malcolm X one morning in 2005 on National Public Radio. This is the boy, now young man, who'd set the fire that killed Malcolm's widow, Dr. Betty Shabazz, in 1997, when he was just twelve years old. Malcolm X had been my hero ever since I was in high school, and my devotion to learning more about him continued into my college years. When I was growing up in the Deep South, the Reverend Martin Luther King, Jr., had been the primary focus of civil rights history taught in the classroom. Reading *The Autobiography of Malcolm X* by Alex Haley at the age of seventeen was one of the most eye-opening experiences of my life. For years I could quote even the most intense Malcolm statements and many other little known facts about the slain Black Muslim leader.

Over the years, I'd spoken at length with Dr. Shabazz, who'd struggled to raise her five daughters on her own and without the support of the mainstream community. Only in the early nineties did the teachings and importance of Malcolm X resonate in the mainstream, culminating with Spike Lee's monumental film. The death of Dr. Shabazz at the hands of her grandson had always seemed a very painful end to a heartbreaking journey for the Shabazz family.

But I felt much hope when I heard the interviews of the

then twenty-year-old Shabazz, who seemed clear and focused, thoughtful and informed. I wanted to know more,
particularly since he was behind bars at the time for a crime
not related to the death of his grandmother. Shabazz had
been a juvenile when he was charged with starting the fire
that killed his grandmother and was released when he was
seventeen years old. Unfortunately, he was arrested for robbery a year later, and this time he was housed in an adult
prison. Clearly, the weight of all that he'd been through had
taken a great toll.

I wanted to know how or if this kid had dealt with the
guilt of his grandmother's death, the weight of being named
after his famous grandfather, and what his future might
hold given that the seriousness of his crimes would no doubt
follow him his entire life. Shabazz was being held at the
Clinton Correctional Facility in upstate New York, a prison
famous for housing Tupac Shakur and for being the current
home of the rapper Shyne. To get there, I had to take two
flights from New York, rent a car to drive through the
mountains, and then board a ferry to the island where the
prison was situated. It took nearly two days to arrive, but I
was prepared with the right pen, notebook, and bra.

I'm not sure what I expected of Malcolm X's grandson.
Malcolm himself had by all accounts been a towering man—
over six feet, with a handsome face and a commanding presence. His grandson was quite the opposite. His slight build
and limited height, along with his delicate features, made
him seem even younger than his twenty years. Even in the
worst of moments, I couldn't imagine anyone thinking that
he would set a fire intentionally to kill his grandmother.

After the guard grilled Shabazz about prison procedures

for an interview, the young man slowly began to reveal the hell he'd been through since that fatal night at his grandmother's apartment. He admitted that he'd never anticipated her running back into the apartment to find him. He'd hoped that his setting the fire would make his grandmother allow him to return to the care of his mother.

"I just wanted to be with my mother, and I thought if I made my grandmother mad enough, she'd just give up and send me back," he explained. Described by psychologists who've examined and worked with him as "brilliant but disturbed," Shabazz also talked honestly about his love for his grandmother and how their closeness had given him comfort after her death. "Me and my grandmother were tighter than tight. Anyone who thinks that I would intentionally hurt her didn't know us very well. I was crazy about her and she was crazy about me. We had the best relationship."

Shabazz's mother had her own problems raising the boy, which had led to his grandmother's intervention. "My grandmother would always step in when my mother couldn't really deal too much—she was always there for me," he said. The young man then began to discuss the trauma of spending most of his childhood behind bars and the way other prisoners treated him. After all, he was the grandson of one of the most famous prisoners ever, which got him instant respect. Some fellow prisoners offered gifts of cigarettes and magazines, while most just let him be. "It was sort of uncomfortable because I didn't really want to be singled out like that. But I knew what my grandfather meant to so many of the guys in here, so I couldn't really just blow off the support."

Shabazz, who has spent a third of his life incarcerated, added that his time behind bars had given him the opportunity to study his grandfather's work in a way that would not have been possible had he been on the outside. "You know, I could really, really relate to the stuff he'd gone through. As a kid, my grandmother didn't talk a lot about my grandfather to me. I think she believed I was too young to understand, but she would tell me jokes about how he hated to smile because he had a gap in his teeth and after he got them fixed, he would just stand in front of the bathroom mirror looking at his new smile. She thought that was funny."

But by far the most painful aspect of our talk was his admission that many of his aunts, Malcolm and Betty's daughters, had not forgiven him for causing their mother's death. They hadn't spoken to him since he'd been in jail, even though he'd attempted to reach out many times via letters. However, a smile lit up his face when he spoke of his aunt Malika, who'd called him on her cell phone from the Malcolm X eightieth birthday celebration. "She wanted me to be included so she always tries to find a way for me to be a part."

His goal upon release, Shabazz said, is to make amends with the aunts who had been his main source of support before the incident. He would also like to continue his grandfather's work by helping the poor and working with young men who are wrongly imprisoned. He was released from prison in 2006 but continues to have unfortunate brushes with the law, which is typical for a child who has spent much of his life behind bars. Sitting in front of this fragile young man had brought full circle the legacy of

Malcolm X to me in many ways. A description on paper of Malcolm's amazing life cannot explain the pain and destruction that were left behind on February 21, 1965, when he was gunned down in front of his wife and young children.

Indeed, Malcolm X's family was emotionally and financially unprepared to face the future without him. In contrast to Martin Luther King, Jr.'s family, who remained visible after his death, Betty Shabazz often had to receive welfare to make ends meet. As a result, though Malcolm Shabazz did not witness his grandfather's violent end, he did inherit the anger, violence, and dysfunction that resulted from a death never fully dealt with by his family or this country. The hope is that young Malcolm Shabazz, after he serves his time, will have the opportunity to carry on his grandfather's mission of reaching back and helping others. His grandparents would be proud.

14

The Players Club

A BEHIND-CLOSED-DOORS WORLD WHERE
HOLLYWOOD, HIP-HOP, AND SPORTS
"MAKE IT RAIN"

Diahnn used to wait tables at Denny's in the yuppie Buckhead section of Atlanta. On nights she wasn't serving French fries and burgers until the wee hours, she was playing hostess at a Spanish eatery just north of Lenox Mall. A tight schedule, given that the twenty-five-year-old single mother of one was also a junior at Georgia State University studying to become an English teacher. But one day Diahnn decided she'd had enough of the $7.50 an hour wages, inconsistent tips, and lousy patron attitudes. She quit without giving two-weeks' notice.

Friends questioned her quick decision, particularly since her seven-year-old son's private school tuition, as well as her own, was due soon, not to mention her $750 a month rent. But Diahnn had a plan, and it's an idea that's rising in popularity with young women in the Atlanta area and a growing number of other cities across the country—exotic dancing. In an era when songs such as "I'm in Love with a Stripper" rule the airwaves and stripper poles are the norm in the homes on any *MTV Cribs* episode featuring a rapper or an athlete, the world of exotic dancing has become more and more en vogue and increasingly enticing to young women, particularly African American women needing quick money and instant validation.

Music videos showcase 24/7 images of barely clothed women sliding across the floor as they seductively dance to please adoring men. Films such as *The Players Club* and *Hustle & Flow* make stripper life seem as normal as any respectable nine-to-five gig, while the comedian Chris Rock has even joked in his stand-up routine, "I'm just trying to keep my daughters off the pole. If I can do that, I've fulfilled my fatherly duties." Rock's two daughters are ages two and four.

Yet as the 2006 rape scandal at Duke University exposes the ugly downside of exotic dancing in clubs and at private parties, many of the young women who undress to pay the bills insist it's worth the risk. "Anything I do can cause me trouble," says Diahnn, who also danced at Magic City, the most famous stripper operation in the South. "I knew coming in that nothing is free and making the kind of money I make would mean I have to lose something along the way. That's the deal."

Losing something is how Diahnn describes the moments she's onstage disrobing down to nothing in front of complete strangers each night. On the nights she dances during the week, she easily gets five hundred dollars or more, and that allows her just to float away onstage as her body moves to the music. "I go into a trance really, I think about my son's smile or his laugh," says Diahnn, a strikingly attractive woman with long hair, flawless mocha skin, and deeply set dimples. "That's the way I get through it because I'm doing this so he can have a better life and I can get the life I want us both to have right now. I know it's worth it in the end."

A native of Nashville, Diahnn learned she was pregnant with her son when she was eighteen and about to start her first year at a junior college in her hometown. Her parents urged her to give the baby up for adoption, but Diahnn was in love with his father and thought they'd build a life together. Nine months later, the father was MIA, leaving Diahnn with two mouths to feed. She had to make a move. "I had a lot of friends who'd come to Atlanta to go to school and then got into stripping on the side," she says. "They made it seem so fly. They talked about all the ballers, rappers, and famous men who would come in and shower them with money each night. At first I was trying to do it the right way—but waiting tables was just causing me and my son to scrape by each month. I couldn't afford to pay someone to watch him." While Diahnn's mother is aware of her night job, her father and her brother, who is studying to become a minister, have no idea.

Indeed, predominantly minority strip clubs like Magic City and the Blue Flame in Atlanta, Club Madonna in Miami, and Paradise in Los Angeles all attract the wealthiest of young men each night, enriched by careers in music, sports, and other high-paying fields. Herman Harris, a manager at Magic City, says the rise of wealth in men between the ages of sixteen and thirty, who routinely "make it rain" (referring to the ritual in which customers throw fistfuls of cash into the air), has fueled the recent explosion of interest in strippers and caused an ever-growing number of younger women to come knocking on his door. "I've definitely seen a rise in college girls in the last three years," says Harris. "It used to be we'd have a lot of women who were older, in their thirties with other lives and day jobs. But now, because of hip-hop music and the big-time money you can make, all the young girls are trying to get their moment."

Harris and other club managers in the Atlanta area estimated at the time of this writing that 10 to 15 percent of the girls who dance at their clubs are college students, almost double the proportion of five years ago. In Los Angeles, club promoters say nearly 10 percent of dancers are college students, and they expect that number to continue to rise. But with youth come problems, and according to Harris, younger women take bigger risks on and off the stage in the hope of bigger paydays and regular side work. "The younger the girls, the harder it is to get them to understand that this is business, that there are rules and people have to follow them or something goes wrong," says Harris. "We always tell the girls if they're going to do outside stuff, they have to take security with them, but most of them don't listen. They have to pay security out of their cut, and they want all their money. Here at the club there is no touching—we make sure of that."

Clubs routinely advise girls not to communicate with patrons after hours and to have someone escort them to and from the club. They are told to resist too much eye contact, even with regular customers. Like Diahnn, Denise dances to pay her bills while she attends California State University, Northridge, in Los Angeles. But paying her bills isn't all she gets from the strip club. Talent agents and casting directors routinely drop by and choose some of the women for videos, movies, and private parties with celebrities. Denise appeared in Ying Yang Twins and Eminem videos last year.

The twenty-two-year-old also says she sometimes dances at private functions, such as bachelor parties, birthday parties, and frat parties to make additional money, but she draws the line at performing for people she doesn't know. A private party can bring a dancer five hundred to a thousand dollars plus tips. "I really have to know the people or be going with a girl that knows them," says Denise. "Otherwise it's a no-go because I know the situations you can get into that you can't get out of, like the one at Duke. It's easy to walk into something like that."

Both Denise and Diahnn say they've stripped at parties for both black and white clients and maintain the attitudes are much more different than people might expect. "When it's a group of all white men, drunk and young, they really get aggressive and lose it," says Denise. "I also think they have less respect for black women because of what they've seen on TV or heard. It's like they think they can do or say things to us they can't with other women. Black guys are usually more laid-back about it. They don't just go nuts because a naked woman is in the room. They enjoy, but it's not the same thing." Neither woman had heard racial insults while dancing.

Daisy, age thirty-three, stripped for five years at a variety of clubs in the Los Angeles area and says that mainstream society's attitudes toward African American women may have played a big factor in the Duke scandal, and those attitudes forced her to quit the business sooner than she'd planned. "I think black women are seen as the lowest of the low in society. We don't count, so why not violate us?" says Daisy, who now works as a paralegal. "I saw that attitude in the club when white customers would come in. They would make me feel really dirty, and that's not how I normally felt up there. I'd be cool when I left the stage, unless a white man was up-front and center looking at me in a way that sent chills up my spine."

Epilogue
A JOURNEY FULL CIRCLE

A Tribute to Coretta Scott King

I began this journey reflecting on the past thirteen years of covering some of the world's most famous people by traveling back to the first story I had ever published, about the legendary film director Francis Ford Coppola. Since I began with a film icon, I thought it would be more than appropriate to end with an icon for the ages—Coretta Scott King.

My first internship, with the *Atlanta Journal-Constitution* in the late eighties, was slow going when I and eleven other students from across the country reported for work. But two weeks in, when the editors had figured out each of our strong points, I was assigned a story on a single mothers' program supported by none other than Mrs. King herself. The assignment would involve interviewing several of the young mothers being assisted by the program on a Saturday morning and conclude with my talking with Mrs. King about her role in the event.

I, like most children of the seventies, grew up with larger-than-life images of the King family throughout our Georgia home. I can still feel the velvety texture of a colorful wall-length mural my grandmother had hanging in her dining room, featuring the images of King, President Kennedy, and Robert Kennedy in a re-creation of the Last Supper. Furniture would come and go from her home, but that mural never left its place until my grandmother's death in 1997. The opportunity to meet the wife of one of the most influential men of our lifetime was an honor I could never have expected so soon in my career.

My nerves were raw as an assistant led me to an office where Mrs. King was waiting for my arrival. The room was a cheery yellow, with beautiful paintings of flowers and water streams, shabby chic—like, if there was such a thing back then. Mrs. King was seated in the middle of the room, wearing a fitted red suit and shiny black pumps. Her hair was in her signature flowing style, and her makeup was as flawless as that of any model ready for her close-up. I somehow managed to get two or three questions out of my mouth before Mrs. King caught on to the fact that I was totally and absolutely in awe of her presence.

As if on cue, this amazing lady began to pose and answer the questions I should have been asking for my story. I sat and listened as she rolled off numbers, facts, and the names of White House officials she'd worked with to get the funding she needed and why this program was so near and dear to her heart. After about forty-five minutes of witnessing her conduct her own interview, I stood to bid her farewell and tell her what an honor and pleasure it was to meet her. I could only imagine how pitifully unprepared I must have seemed to this woman who'd been interviewed by some of the world's most respected journalists.

My story ran that Monday and highlighted a pretty important issue in the Atlanta area. I was proud just to get it in the paper. But nothing in my career has meant more than the letter Mrs. King sent to my editor just days after the article ran. In the letter, she complimented me on my professionalism, my preparation, and my insight into such a touching issue. "Her observations resulted in an excellent article in your paper. It revealed to the reader the significant accomplishments made by our Single Parents Program. . . . Again, I commend her assertive style and professionalism. I look forward to hearing more from her in the future," Mrs. King wrote. I'm not sure who Mrs. King met that day, but it sure wasn't me!

But while I didn't fully realize it then, what she'd done for me and other African American writers with that letter was to alert the newspaper to the need to see more faces like mine doing what I was doing. She also did it to inspire and encourage me to keep working at my job until the day I wouldn't be awestruck and clueless anymore, until the day I would actually be good. It worked.

As the one-year anniversary of the death of this great woman approaches, I felt it was only fair and fitting to dedicate this book to her and her lifelong struggle to see that equality wasn't just a dream but a reality.

© IAN GITTLER

ALLISON SAMUELS has been a correspondent in *Newsweek*'s Los Angeles bureau since September 1996. She covers sports and entertainment, and has recently interviewed personalities such as Disney star Raven Symone, Jada Pinkett Smith, and Oscar-nominated actor Terrence Howard. In the midst of the Kobe Bryant rape allegation scandal, Samuels penned a *Newsweek* cover story that garnered so much national attention that she was a guest on the *Today* show and *Larry King Live*, among nearly two hundred other radio and television interviews. Samuels shared a 1997 National Association of Black Journalists Award for *Newsweek*'s March 17, 1997, cover package "Black Like Who?" which she coauthored with John Leland, Ellis Cose, and Vern Smith. She is a member of the National Association of Black Journalists, the Big Sisters of America, and the UCLA Black Studies Department board of directors. Samuels is also a regular entertainment contributor for National Public Radio.